100 Favorite
English and Irish
Poems

DOVER · THRIFT · EDITIONS

100 Favorite English and Irish Poems

Edited by

CLARENCE C. STROWBRIDGE

DOVER PUBLICATIONS, INC.
Mineola, New York

DOVER THRIFT EDITIONS

GENERAL EDITOR: MARY CAROLYN WALDREP
EDITOR OF THIS VOLUME: CLARENCE C. STROWBRIDGE

ACKNOWLEDGMENTS: see page vii.

Bibliographical Note

100 Favorite English and Irish Poems is a new work, first published by Dover
Publications, Inc., in 2006.

Library of Congress Cataloging-in-Publication Data

100 favorite English and Irish poems / edited by Clarence C. Strowbridge.
    p. cm. — (Dover thrift editions)
    ISBN-13: 978-0-486-44429-1
    ISBN-10: 0-486-44429-5
    1. English poetry. I. Title: One hundred favorite English and Irish poems.
II. Strowbridge, Clarence C. III. Series.

PR1175.A137144 2006
821.008—dc22

     2005051876

Manufactured in the United States by RR Donnelley
44429504   2015
www.doverpublications.com

Note

While there are many great English and Irish poems and poets, this hand-picked selection includes 100 of the most beloved poems in this category by fifty-nine well-known poets. The poems have been arranged in chronological order, ranging from the late Middle Ages through the 1940s (with the exception of Sir Walter Raleigh's response to Christopher Marlowe's *The Passionate Shepherd to His Love*), allowing one to see the progression of poetry, its themes and concerns, throughout four centuries.

The majority of the works in this collection are by English poets who were inspired by politics and religion, love and war, and the natural beauty of their country. During the Elizabethan era (1558–1603), litera-ture and music flourished as Thomas Campion and Thomas Nashe composed songs to entertain royalty; courtiers Sir Walter Raleigh and Sir Phillip Sidney paid homage to the queen with their poems; and William Shakespeare created masques for the court's pleasure. Emerging from the English Renaissance (early sixteenth through the mid-seventeenth cen-tury) was the Metaphysical imagery of George Herbert and John Donne, and the secular verse of the Cavalier poets, Sir John Suckling and Robert Herrick. The Restoration of 1660 was dominated by the doctrine of skepticism revealed in the satirical works of John Dryden and Alexander Pope. Lord Byron and William Wordsworth, poets of the Romantic Movement (1789–1824), focused their poetic energies on nature and the art of personal expression. The Victorian poetry of Alfred, Lord Tennyson and Robert Browning highlighted important social, economic, and polit-ical issues of their time. Pre-Raphaelites Christina Rossetti and William Morris returned to a medieval type of imagery, while Georgians D. H. Lawrence and Rupert Brooke preferred romanticism. Some poets like Wilfred Owen and Isaac Rosenberg experienced firsthand the horrors of World War I and articulated their fears and concerns in verse (and many of them, unfortunately, died in battle). Modernist T. S. Eliot was an inno-vator and experimented with form and style. During the 1930s, when

England was in a state of upheaval, the poetry of W. H. Auden and
Stephen Spender began to take a political turn.

Also represented in this anthology are works by William Butler Yeats,
winner of the Nobel Prize for Literature in 1923; Robert Burns,
Scotland's national poet; and Dylan Thomas, a leading figure in Anglo-
Welsh literature. And there are other renowned poets from Ireland and
the British Isles included here to complete this overview of some of the
most popular poems ever written in the English language.

Acknowledgments

W. H. Auden: "Musée des Beaux Arts," from *Collected Poems*. Copyright © 1940 and renewed 1968 by W. H. Auden. Reprinted by permission of Faber and Faber Ltd. and Random House, Inc.

Walter de la Mare: "The Listeners" from *The Complete Poems of Walter de la Mare*. Reprinted by permission of the Literary Trustees of Walter de la Mare and the Society of Authors as their representative.

T. S. Eliot: "Sweeney Among the Nightingales" from *Collected Poems 1909–1962*. Reprinted by permission of Faber and Faber Ltd.

Robert Graves: "When I'm Killed" from *Collected Poems*. Reprinted by permission of Carcanet Press Limited.

A. E. Housman: "To an Athlete Dying Young," "Loveliest of Trees," and "When I Was One-and-Twenty" from *The Collected Poems of A. E. Housman*. Reprinted by permission of the Society of Authors as the Literary Representative of the Estate of A. E. Housman.

John Masefield: "Cargoes" and "Sea Fever" from *The Sea Poems*. Reprinted by permission of the Society of Authors as the Literary Representative of the Estate of John Masefield.

Stephen Spender: "I Think Continually of Those Who Were Truly Great" from *New Collected Poems*. Copyright © 2004 by Stephen Spender. Reprinted by permission of the Estate of Sir Stephen Spender.

Dylan Thomas: "Do Not Go Gentle into That Good Night" from *The Poems of Dylan Thomas*. Copyright © 1952 by Dylan Thomas. Reprinted by permission of New Directions Publishing Corp.

William Butler Yeats: "The Wild Swans at Coole" and "Easter 1916" from *The Collected Poems of W. B. Yeats*. Reprinted by permission of A. P. Watt, Ltd., on behalf of Michael B. Yeats.

Contents

Isaac Rosenberg (1890–1918)

Returning, We Hear the Larks

Anthem for Doomed Youth 80

Robert Graves (1895–1985)

When I'm Killed 81

W. H. Auden (1907–1973)

Musée des Beaux Arts 82

Stephen Spender (1909–1995)

I Think Continually of Those Who Were Truly Great 83

Do Not Go Gentle into That Good Night 84

Alphabetical List of Titles 85

Alphabetical List of First Lines 88

100 Favorite
English and Irish
Poems

ANONYMOUS (Late Middle Ages)

Ballads are anonymous, frequently tragic, storytelling songs that often developed for centuries before being recorded in writing. The following are two of the most famous English ballads, dating probably from the late Middle Ages.

Lord Randal

"O where hae ye been, Lord Randal, my son?
O where hae ye been, my handsome young man?"
"I hae been to the wild wood; mother, make my bed soon,
For I'm weary wi' hunting, and fain wald lie down."

"Where gat ye your dinner, Lord Randal, my son?
Where gat ye your dinner, my handsome young man?"
"I din'd wi' my true-love; mother, make my bed soon,
For I'm weary wi' hunting, and fain wald lie down."

"What gat ye to your dinner, Lord Randal, my son?
What gat ye to your dinner, my handsome young man?"
"I gat eels boil'd in broo;[1] mother, make my bed soon,
For I'm weary wi' hunting, and fain wald lie down."

"What became of your bloodhounds, Lord Randal, my son?
What became of your bloodhounds, my handsome young man?"
"O they swell'd and they died; mother, make my bed soon,
For I'm weary wi' hunting, and fain wald lie down."

"O I fear ye are poison'd, Lord Randal, my son!
I fear ye are poison'd, my handsome young man!"
"O yes! I am poison'd; mother, make my bed soon,
For I'm sick at the heart, and fain wald lie down."

---

[1]*broo*] broth.

Sir Patrick Spens

I. THE SAILING

The king sits in Dunfermline town
  Drinking the blude-red[1] wine;
"O whare will I get a skeely[2] skipper
  To sail this new ship o' mine?"

O up and spak an eldern knight,
  Sat at the king's right knee;
"Sir Patrick Spens is the best sailor
  That ever sail'd the sea."

Our king has written a braid[3] letter,
  And seal'd it with his hand,
And sent it to Sir Patrick Spens,
  Was walking on the strand.

"To Noroway, to Noroway,
  To Noroway o'er the faem;[4]
The king's daughter o' Noroway,
  'Tis thou must bring her hame."

The first word that Sir Patrick read
  So loud, loud laugh'd he;
The neist[5] word that Sir Patrick read
  The tear blinded his e'e.

"O wha is this has done this deed
  And tauld the king o' me,
To send us out, at this time o' year,
  To sail upon the sea?

"Be it wind, be it weet,[6] be it hail, be it sleet,
  Our ship must sail the faem;
The king's daughter o' Noroway,
  'Tis we must fetch her hame."

---

[1] *blude-red*] blood-red.
[2] *skeely*] skillful.
[3] *braid*] broad.
[4] *faem*] foam.
[5] *neist*] next.
[6] *weet*] wet.

They hoysed[7] their sails on Monenday morn
  Wi' a' the speed they may;
They hae landed in Noroway
  Upon a Wodensday.

II. THE RETURN

"Mak ready, mak ready, my merry men a'!
  Our gude[8] ship sails the morn."
"Now ever alack, my master dear,
  I fear a deadly storm.

"I saw the new moon late yestreen[9]
  Wi' the auld moon in her arm;
And if we gang to sea, master,
  I fear we'll come to harm."

They hadna sail'd a league, a league,
  A league but barely three,
When the lift[10] grew dark, and the wind blew loud,
  And gurly[11] grew the sea.

The ankers brak, and the topmast lap,[12]
  It was sic a deadly storm:
And the waves cam owre the broken ship
  Till a' her sides were torn.

"Go fetch a web o' the silken claith,
  Another o' the twine,
And wap them into our ship's side,
  And let nae the sea come in."

They fetch'd a web o' the silken claith,
  Another o' the twine,
And they wapp'd them round that gude ship's side,
  But still the sea came in.

---

[7] *hoysed*] hoisted.
[8] *gude*] good.
[9] *yestreen*] yesterday evening.
[10] *lift*] sky.
[11] *gurly*] grim, surly.
[12] *lap*] leaped.

O laith,[13] laith were our gude Scots lords
    To wet their cork-heel'd shoon;[14]
But lang or a' the play was play'd
    They wat their hats aboon.[15]

And mony was the feather bed
    That flatter'd[16] on the faem;
And mony was the gude lord's son
    That never mair cam hame.

O lang, lang may the ladies sit,
    Wi' their fans into their hand,
Before they see Sir Patrick Spens
    Come sailing to the strand!

And lang, lang may the maidens sit
    Wi' their gowd kames[17] in their hair,
A-waiting for their ain dear loves!
    For them they'll see nae mair.

Half-owre,[18] half-owre to Aberdour,
    'Tis fifty fathoms deep;
And there lies gude Sir Patrick Spens,
    Wi' the Scots lords at his feet!

EDMUND SPENSER (1552?–1599)

The complex rhyme scheme of Elizabethan poet Edmund Spenser was an inspiration to poets like Keats, Lord Byron, Shelley, and others. The Spenserian sonnet can be found throughout his major work, *The Faerie Queene* (1596), and in the following stanza from *Amoretti* (1595), a sequence of eighty-eight sonnets dedicated to the lady who eventually became his wife.

Sonnet 75

One day I wrote her name upon the strand,
But came the waves and washèd it away:
Agayne I wrote it with a second hand,

---

[13] *laith*] loath.
[14] *shoon*] shoes.
[15] *aboon*] above.
[16] *flatter'd*] floated.
[17] *gowd kames*] gold combs.
[18] *half-owre*] halfway.

But came the tyde, and made my paynes his pray.[1]
"Vayne man," sayd she, "that doest in vaine assay,
A mortall thing so to immortalize,
For I my selve shall lyke to this decay,
And eek[2] my name bee wypèd out lykewize."
"Not so," quod[3] I, "let baser things devize,
To dy in dust, but you shall live by fame:
My verse your vertues rare shall eternize,
And in the heavens wryte your glorious name.
Where whenas death shall all the world subdew,
Our love shall live, and later life renew."

SIR PHILIP SIDNEY (1554–1586)

This Renaissance poet was a leading member of Queen Elizabeth's court, a
statesman, and a soldier. He fought in the war against Spain and received a fatal
wound during the battle at Zutphen at age thirty-two. The following verse is
from one of the great sonnet sequences *Astrophil and Stella* (ca. 1581), which was
published posthumously.

Sonnet 1

Loving in truth, and fain in verse my love to show,
That the dear she might take some pleasure of my pain,
Pleasure might cause her read, reading might make her know,
Knowledge might pity win, and pity grace obtain,
    I sought fit words to paint the blackest face of woe:
Studying inventions fine, her wits to entertain,
Oft turning others' leaves, to see if thence would flow
Some fresh and fruitful showers upon my sunburned brain.
    But words came halting forth, wanting Invention's stay;
Invention, Nature's child, fled step-dame Study's blows,
And others' feet still seemed but strangers in my way.
Thus great with child to speak, and helpless in my throes,
    Biting my trewand[1] pen, beating myself for spite,
    "Fool," said my Muse to me, "look in thy heart and write."

---

[1] *pray*] prey.
[2] *eek*] also.
[3] *quod*] quoth.

---

[1] *trewand*] truant.

CHRISTOPHER MARLOWE (1564–1593)

Second only to Shakespeare (whom he inspired) as an Elizabethan dramatist, Marlowe penned some of the earliest and greatest English-language tragedies before being killed in a tavern at age twenty-nine.

The Passionate Shepherd to His Love

Come live with me and be my Love,
And we will all the pleasures prove
That hills and valleys, dales and fields,
Or woods or steepy mountain yields.

And we will sit upon the rocks,
And see the shepherds feed their flocks
By shallow rivers, to whose falls
Melodious birds sing madrigals.

And I will make thee beds of roses
And a thousand fragrant posies;
A cap of flowers, and a kirtle
Embroider'd all with leaves of myrtle.

A gown made of the finest wool
Which from our pretty lambs we pull;
Fair-lined slippers for the cold,
With buckles of the purest gold.

A belt of straw and ivy-buds
With coral clasps and amber studs:
And if these pleasures may thee move,
Come live with me and be my Love.

The shepherd swains shall dance and sing
For thy delight each May morning:
If these delights thy mind may move,
Then live with me and be my Love.

SIR WALTER RALEIGH (1552–1618)

Raleigh was a poet, writer, explorer, and was a favorite of Queen Elizabeth until he had an affair with one of her ladies-in-waiting. He composed one of his greatest works, *History of the World* (1614), while imprisoned in the Tower of London by King James for treason. He was eventually executed before its completion. The following is a poem he wrote in response to Marlowe's *The Passionate Shepherd to His Love*.

The Nymph's Reply to the Shepherd

If all the world and love were young,
And truth in every shepherd's tongue,
These pretty pleasures might me move
To live with thee and be thy love.

Time drives the flocks from field to fold
When rivers rage and rocks grow cold,
And Philomel[1] becometh dumb;
The rest complains of cares to come.

The flowers do fade, and wanton fields
To wayward winter reckoning yields;
A honey tongue, a heart of gall,
Is fancy's spring, but sorrow's fall.

Thy gowns, thy shoes, thy beds of roses,
Thy cap, thy kirtle,[2] and thy posies
Soon break, soon wither, soon forgotten—
In folly ripe, in reason rotten.

Thy belt of straw and ivy buds,
Thy coral clasps and amber studs,
All these in me no means can move
To come to thee and be thy love.

But could youth last and love still breed,
Had joys no date[3] nor age no need,
Then these delights my mind might move
To live with thee and be thy love.

---

[1] *Philomel*] the nightingale.
[2] *kirtle*] skirt, outer petticoat.
[3] *date*] ending.

WILLIAM SHAKESPEARE (1564–1616)

The preeminent English poet and playwright, Shakespeare published a sequence of 154 sonnets in 1609 that continues to be regarded as the highest perfection of the form in English. Selected are four of these sonnets covering such themes as beauty, loss and sorrow, age, and soul, plus a song from *Cymbeline* (ca. 1609), one of Shakespeare's late romances.

Fear No More the Heat o' the Sun

Fear no more the heat o' the sun,
    Nor the furious winter's rages;
Thou thy worldly task hast done,
    Home art gone, and ta'en thy wages.
Golden lads and girls all must,
As chimney-sweepers, come to dust.

Fear no more the frown o' the great;
    Thou art past the tyrant's stroke;
Care no more to clothe and eat;
    To thee the reed is as the oak:
The scepter, learning, physic, must
All follow this, and come to dust.

Fear no more the lightning flash,
    Nor the all-dreaded thunder stone;
Fear not slander, censure rash;
    Thou hast finished joy and moan:
All lovers young, all lovers must
Consign to thee, and come to dust.

No exorciser harm thee!
Nor no witchcraft charm thee!
Ghost unlaid forbear thee!
Nothing ill come near thee!
Quiet consummation have;
And renownèd be thy grave!

Sonnet 18

Shall I compare thee to a summer's day?
Thou art more lovely and more temperate:
Rough winds do shake the darling buds of May,
And summer's lease hath all too short a date:

In me thou see'st the glowing of such fire, *his life is dying*
That on the ashes of his youth doth lie,
As the death-bed whereon it must expire, *the very light that*
Consumed with that which it was nourish'd by. *nourished him is killing him*
  This thou perceivest, which makes thy love more strong,
  To love that well which thou must leave ere long. *should love now more than ever*

Sonnet 146

Poor soul, the center of my sinful earth, *soul/reason behind sin*
Lord of these rebel powers that thee array,
Why dost thou pine within and suffer dearth,
Painting thy outward walls so costly gay?
Why so large cost, having so short a lease, *why is life short, yet so much*
Dost thou upon thy fading mansion spend? *is expected by*
Shall worms, inheritors of this excess, *— We end up in the ground*
Eat up thy charge? Is this thy body's end? *anyways*
Then, soul, live thou upon thy servant's loss,
And let that pine to aggravate thy store;
Buy terms divine in selling hours of dross;
Within be fed, without be rich no more.
personification
  So shalt thou feed on death, that feeds on men, *death is dead*
  And death once dead, there's no more dying then. *when there is no more dying*

THOMAS NASHE (1567–1601)

During a tempestuous and brief career, Nashe produced plays, satire, pamphlets, and a novel, as well as poetry. The following lyric is taken from his comedy *Summer's Last Will and Testament* (1592).

Adieu, Farewell Earth's Bliss

Adieu, farewell earth's bliss;
This world uncertain is;
Fond are life's lustful joys;
Death proves them all but toys; *Joys = unnecessary*
None from his darts can fly; *Death = unavoidable*
I am sick, I must die.
  Lord, have mercy on us!

Sometime too hot the eye of heaven shines,
And often is his gold complexion dimm'd;
And every fair from fair sometime declines,
By chance or nature's changing course untrimm'd;
But thy eternal summer shall not fade, ← *never lose the*
Nor lose possession of that fair thou owest;
Nor shall Death brag thou wander'st in his shade,
When in eternal lines to time thou grow'st:
  So long as men can breathe, or eyes can see,
  So long lives this, and this gives life to thee. *this "" is beauty*

Sonnet 30

sitting of court
When to the sessions of sweet silent thought
I summon up remembrance of things past,
I sigh the lack of many a thing I sought,
And with old woes new wail my dear time's waste: *wishing past away*
Then can I drown an eye (unused to flow)
For precious friends hid in death's dateless[1] night,
And weep afresh love's long since canceled woe, *sorrow over lost friends*
And moan th' expense of many a vanished sight: *all the things she's experienced*
Then can I grieve at grievances foregone,
And heavily from woe to woe tell o'er
The sad account of fore-bemoanèd moan,
Which I new pay as if not paid before.
  But if the while I think on thee, dear friend, *twist*
  All losses are restored and sorrows end. *sadness is temporary*

Sonnet 73

That time of year thou mayst in me behold *= mid fall*
When yellow leaves, or none, or few, do hang
Upon those boughs which shake against the cold,
Bare ruin'd choirs, where late the sweet birds sang.
In me thou see'st the twilight of such day *He is as worn as the season*
As after sunset fadeth in the west;
Which by and by black night doth take away, *loses himself more*
Death's second self, that seals up all in rest.

---

[1] *dateless*] endless.

Rich men, trust not in wealth,
Gold cannot buy you health;
Physic himself must fade.

Warning that no money will stop death

All things to end are made,
The plague full swift goes by;
I am sick, I must die.
    Lord, have mercy on us!

Everything is made to die

Beauty is but a flower
Which wrinkles will devour;
Brightness falls from the air;
Queens have died young and fair;
Dust hath closed Helen's eye.
I am sick, I must die.
    Lord, have mercy on us!

Beauty is only destroyed by time

Strength stoops unto the grave,
Worms feed on Hector brave;
Swords may not fight with fate,
Earth still holds ope her gate.
"Come, come," the bells do cry.
I am sick, I must die.
    Lord, have mercy on us!

Death even eats strength
No amount of strength can stop fate

Wit with his wantonness
Tasteth death's bitterness;
Hell's executioner
Hath no ears for to hear
What vain art can reply.
I am sick, I must die.
    Lord, have mercy on us!

Nothing said will stop death

Haste, therefore, each degree,
To welcome destiny;
Heaven is our heritage,
Earth but a player's stage;
Mount we unto the sky.
I am sick, I must die.
    Lord, have mercy on us!

Just accept death

THOMAS CAMPION (1567–1620)

Campion was a physician, law student, and the only great English poet-composer. He set his lyrics to music and published five volumes of poems with lute accompaniment. This poem can be found in the *Third and Fourth Booke of Ayres* (1617).

There Is a Garden in Her Face

There is a garden in her face,
Where roses and white lilies grow,
A heavenly paradise is that place,
Wherein all pleasant fruits do flow.
There cherries grow, which none may buy
Till "Cherry ripe!"[1] themselves do cry.

Those cherries fairly do enclose
Of orient pearl a double row;
Which when her lovely laughter shows,
They look like rosebuds filled with snow.
Yet them nor peer nor prince can buy,
Till "Cherry ripe!" themselves do cry.

Her eyes like angels watch them still;
Her brows like bended bows do stand,
Threatening with piercing frowns to kill
All that attempt with eye or hand
Those sacred cherries to come nigh,
Till "Cherry ripe!" themselves do cry.

JOHN DONNE (1572?–1631)

Born a Catholic, Donne became an Anglican cleric of great influence. He also wrote secular, as well as religious poetry that combined brilliant craftsmanship, heartfelt emotion, and intellectual rigor while addressing issues of love and faith.

The Good Morrow

I wonder by my troth, what thou, and I
Did, till we lov'd? were we not wean'd till then?
But suck'd on country pleasures, childishly?

---

[1] "*Cherry ripe!*"] a familiar cry of London street vendors.

Or snorted we in the seven sleepers' den?
'Twas so; but this, all pleasures fancies be.
If ever any beauty I did see,
Which I desir'd, and got, 'twas but a dream of thee. ⎤ New love

And now good morrow to our waking souls,
Which watch not one another out of fear;
For love, all love of other sights controls, — Nothing is above love

And makes one little room, an everywhere.
Let sea-discoverers to new worlds have gone,
Let maps to other, worlds on worlds have shown,
Let us possess one world, each hath one, and is one.

My face in thine eye, thine in mine appears, ⎤ They contain
And true plain hearts do in the faces rest,   ⎦ each other
Where can we find two better hemispheres
Without sharp north, without declining west? ⎦
Whatever dies, was not mix'd equally;
If our two loves be one, or, thou and I
Love so alike, that none do slacken, none can die.

Song

    Go and catch a falling star, A
        Get with child a mandrake root, B
    Tell me where all past years are, A   Go out
        Or who cleft the devil's foot, B   and explore
    Teach me to hear mermaids' singing, C the world
        Or to keep off envy's stinging, C
            And find D
            What wind O
    Serves to advance an honest mind. D

    If thou be'st born to strange sights,
        Things invisible to see,
    Ride ten thousand days and nights,   Learn until you grow
        Till Age snow white hairs on thee; old
    Thou, when thou return'st, wilt tell me
    All strange wonders that befell thee,
            And swear
            No where
    Lives a woman true and fair.

    If thou find'st one, let me know; — Explore for me
        Such a pilgrimage were sweet,

Yet do not; I would not go,
　　Though at next door we might meet.
Though she were true when you met her,
And last till you write your letter,
　　　　Yet she
　　　　Will be
False, ere I come, to two or three.

Holy Sonnet 10

Death, be not proud, though some have called thee *suicide?*
Mighty and dreadful, for, thou art not so,
For, those, whom thou think'st, thou dost overthrow, *challenge death*
Die not, poor death, nor yet canst thou kill me.
From rest and sleep, which but thy pictures be,
Much pleasure, then from thee, much more must flow,
And soonest our best men with thee do go,
Rest of their bones, and soul's delivery. *take care of our best*
Thou art slave to fate, chance, kings, and desperate men,
And dost with poison, war, and sickness dwell,
And poppy, or charms can make us sleep as well,
And better than thy stroke; why swell'st thou then?
One short sleep past, we wake eternally, *Eternal life ends death*
And death shall be no more; death, thou shalt die.

BEN JONSON (1572–1637)

At his peak the leading literary figure of his day, Jonson was an associate of
Shakespeare, Donne, and other distinguished persons, as well as poet laureate. He
was an accomplished playwright, translator, and critic, and also wrote great lyric
poetry.

Song: To Celia

Drink to me, only, with thine eyes, *A*
　　And I will pledge with mine; *B* *Asks for*
Or leave a kiss but in the cup *C* *attention*
　　And I'll not look for wine. *B*
The thirst that from the soul doth rise *A*

Doth ask a drink divine; *B*
But might I of Jove's nectar sup, *C*
    I would not change for thine. *B*

I sent thee late a rosy wreath, *A* gives gifts in return that
    Not so much honouring thee *B* he is forgiven?
As giving it a hope that there *C*
    It could not wither'd be; *B*
But thou thereon didst only breathe, *A*
    And sent'st it back to me; *B* Rejection of communion
Since when it grows, and smells, I swear, *C*
    Not of itself but thee! *B*

ROBERT HERRICK (1591–1674)

One of Ben Jonson's many followers, Herrick did not let his position as an
Anglican cleric deter his composing sensual lyrics (of which the following is a
mild example) that celebrate the earthly pleasures of human existence.

carpe
Diem   ### To the Virgins, to Make Much of Time

Gather ye rosebuds while ye may,
    Old Time is still a-flying: Time is spontaneous, goes by quickly
And this same flower that smiles to-day
    To-morrow will be dying.

The glorious lamp of heaven, the sun, *A*
    The higher he's a-getting, *B*   Day is running out
The sooner will his race be run, *A*
    And nearer he's to setting. *B*

That age is best which is the first,   prime time is great
    When youth and blood are warmer;
But being spent, the worse, and worst ⎤ That time will
    Times still succeed the former. ⎦ pass

Then be not coy, but use your time,
    And while ye may, go marry:
For having lost but once your prime, Don't take time for
    You may for ever tarry.   granted, do as you wish
                                ASAP

GEORGE HERBERT (1593–1633)

Like his contemporary Herrick, an Anglican clergyman, as well as poet, Herbert stood in contrast to the former as a model of virtue, piety, and devotion. The following is Herbert's most famous poem, and is a fine example of metaphysical poetry.

The Pulley

When God at first made man,
Having a glass of blessings standing by,
"Let us," said he, "pour on him all we can:
Let the world's riches, which dispersèd lie,
    Contract into a span."

So strength first made a way;
Then beauty flowed, then wisdom, honor, pleasure.
When almost all was out, God made a stay,
Perceiving that, alone of all his treasure,
    Rest in the bottom lay.

"For if I should," said he,
"Bestow this jewel also on my creature,
He would adore my gifts instead of me,
And rest in Nature, not the God of Nature;
    So both should losers be.

"Yet let him keep the rest,
But keep them with repining restlessness:
Let him be rich and weary, that at least,
If goodness lead him not, yet weariness
    May toss him to my breast."

THOMAS CAREW (1595–1639)

Carew was greatly influenced by Ben Jonson, who was the poet laureate at the time, and John Donne. The following is one of Carew's most popular songs from *Poems* (1640), a volume containing over 100 poems and his only masque *Coelum Brittanicum* (1643).

A Song

Ask me no more where Jove bestows,
When June is past, the fading rose;
For in your beauties orient deep,
These flowers, as in their causes, sleep.

Ask me no more whither do stray
The golden atoms of the day; *stars?*
For in pure love heaven did prepare
Those powders to enrich your hair.

Ask me no more whither doth haste
The nightingale when May is past;
For in your sweet dividing throat
She winters, and keeps warm her note.

Ask me no more where those stars light,
That downwards fall in dead of night;
For in your eyes they sit, and there
Fixèd become, as iF their sphere.

Ask me no more if east or west
The phoenix builds her spicy nest;
For unto you at last she flies,
And in your fragment bosom dies.

EDMUND WALLER (1606–1687)

Waller was a Royalist lawyer and politician whose poetry was first published in
1645 while he was in political exile. He is credited with bringing a new level of
technical mastery to English verse.

Song

Go, lovely Rose— *subject*
Tell her that wastes her time and me,
      That now she knows,
When I resemble her to thee, *Uses subject's beauty to describe*
How sweet and fair she seems to be. *hers*

      Tell her that's young,
And shuns to have her graces spied,
      That hadst thou sprung
In deserts where no men abide,
Thou must have uncommended died.

      Small is the worth
Of beauty from the light retired:
      Bid her come forth,
Suffer herself to be desired, *Enjoy the attention*
And not blush so to be admired.

Then die—that she
The common fate of all things rare
May read in thee;
How small a part of time they share
That are so wondrous sweet and fair!

JOHN MILTON (1608–1674)

Best known as the Puritan author of the epic poem *Paradise Lost,* Milton excelled in short forms as well. His relatively few sonnets include some of the finest in the language.

On His Blindness

When I consider how my light is spent
  Ere half my days in this dark world and wide,
  And that one Talent which is death to hide
  Lodged with me useless, though my soul more bent
To serve therewith my Maker, and present
  My true account, lest He returning chide,
  "Doth God exact day-labour, light denied?"
  I fondly ask. But Patience, to prevent
That murmur, soon replies, "God doth not need
  Either man's work or his own gifts. Who best
  Bear his mild yoke, they serve him best. His state
Is kingly: thousands at his bidding speed,
  And post o'er land and ocean without rest;
  They also serve who only stand and wait."

On His Deceased Wife

Methought I saw my late espousèd saint
  Brought to me like Alcestis from the grave,
  Whom Jove's great son to her glad husband gave,
  Rescued from Death by force, though pale and faint.
Mine, as whom washed from spot of childbed taint
  Purification in the Old Law did save,

And such as yet once more I trust to have
   Full sight of her in Heaven without restraint, *excited to see her again*
Came vested all in white, pure as her mind.
   Her face was veiled; yet to my fancied sight
   Love, sweetness, goodness, in her person shined *she is an angel*
So clear as in no face with more delight.
   But, oh! as to embrace me she inclined,
   I waked, she fled, and day brought back my night. *woke up*

SIR JOHN SUCKLING (1609–1642)

Grouped with Richard Lovelace as a leading "Cavalier" poet (his political involve-
ment forced him to flee the country), Suckling wrote plays and poetry that are
notable for their refinement and polished ease.

Why So Pale and Wan, Fond Lover?

Why so pale and wan, fond lover? *A*
   Prithee, why so pale? *B*
Will, when looking well can't move her, *A*
   Looking ill prevail? *B*
   Prithee, why so pale? *B*

Why so dull and mute, young sinner?
   Prithee, why so mute?
Will, when speaking well can't win her,
   Saying nothing do 't? *Very distant*
   Prithee, why so mute?

Quit, quit for shame! This will not move;
   This cannot take her.
If of herself she will not love, *Her mourning of herself*
   Nothing can make her: *will only take her to hell*
   The devil take her!

RICHARD LOVELACE (1618–1657).

Like Suckling, an active Royalist, Lovelace wrote poems based on his unhappy
experiences, including warfare and imprisonment that combine sentiments of
courtly love with political gallantry.

To Lucasta, Going to the Wars

Tell me not, Sweet, I am unkind,
    That from the nunnery
Of thy chaste breast and quiet mind
    To war and arms I fly.

True, a new mistress now I chase,
    The first foe in the field;
And with a stronger faith embrace
    A sword, a horse, a shield.

Yet this inconstancy is such
    As thou too shalt adore;
I could not love thee, Dear, so much,
    Loved I not Honour more.

To Althea, from Prison

When Love with unconfinèd wings
    Hovers within my gates,
And my divine Althea brings
    To whisper at the grates;
When I lie tangled in her hair
    And fettered to her eye,
The gods that wanton in the air
    Know no such liberty.

When flowing cups run swiftly round,
    With no allaying Thames,
Our careless heads with roses bound,
    Our hearts with loyal flames;
When thirsty grief in wine we steep,
    When healths and draughts go free,
Fishes that tipple in the deep
    Know no such liberty.

When, like committed linnets, I
   With shriller throat shall sing
The sweetness, mercy, majesty,
   And glories of my King;
When I shall voice aloud how good
   He is, how great should be,
Enlargèd wings, that curl the flood,
   Know no such liberty.

Stone walls do not a prison make,
   Nor iron bars a cage;
Minds innocent and quiet take

   That for an hermitage.
If I have freedom in my love,
   And in my soul am free,
Angels alone, that soar above,
   Enjoy such liberty.

HENRY VAUGHAN (1621–1695)

Vaughan was a Welsh physician of hermetic leanings whose verses contain occult
and alchemical themes. Greatly influenced by the more pious George Herbert,
Vaughan was, in turn, a shaping force upon Wordsworth.

The Retreat

Happy those early days! when I
Shined in my angel-infancy.
Before I understood this place
Appointed for my second race,
Or taught my soul to fancy ought
But a white, celestial thought,
When yet I had not walked above
A mile or two, from my first love,
And looking back (at that short space)
Could see a glimpse of his bright face;
When on some *gilded cloud* or *flower*
My gazing soul would dwell an hour,
And in those weaker glories spy
Some shadows of eternity;

Before I taught my tongue to wound ⌐Cursing
My conscience with a sinful sound, ⌐
Or had the black art to dispense
A sev'ral sin to ev'ry sense,
But felt through all this fleshly dress
Bright *shoots* of everlastingness.
  O, how I long to travel back ⌐Throwback
And tread again that ancient track! ⌐
That I might once more reach that plain,
Where first I left my glorious train;
From whence th' inlightened spirit sees
That shady city of palm trees;
But (ah!) my soul with too much stay
Is drunk, and staggers in the way.
Some men a forward motion love,
But I by backward steps would move,
And when this dust falls to the urn ←Death
In that state I came, return. ←only in death can she
      relive life

ANDREW MARVELL (1621–1678)

Better known as a politician than a poet until the twentieth century, Marvell was a Member of Parliament whose greatest works were not published until after his death. "To His Coy Mistress" playfully combines sensuality with more serious themes.

To His Coy Mistress

Had we but world enough, and time, A
This coyness, Lady, were no crime. A
We would sit down and think which way B
To walk and pass our long love's day. B
Thou by the Indian Ganges' side C
Shouldst rubies find: I by the tide C
Of Humber would complain. I would D
Love you ten years before the Flood, D
And you should, if you please, refuse E

But bright Cecilia raised the wonder higher:
When to her organ vocal breath was given,
An angel heard, and straight appeared,
Mistaking earth for heaven.

GRAND CHORUS

As from the power of sacred lays
  The spheres began to move,
And sung the great Creator's praise
  To all the blest above;
So, when the last and dreadful hour
This crumbling pageant shall devour,
The trumpet shall be heard on high,
The dead shall live, the living die,
And Music shall untune the sky.

ALEXANDER POPE (1688–1744)

One of the greatest English poets of the eighteenth century, Alexander Pope was a master of the heroic couplet (a two-line stanza) and had success translating such works as the *Iliad* and the *Odyssey*. Pope was approximately twelve years old when he wrote this poem.

Ode on Solitude

Happy the man whose wish and care
  A few paternal acres bound,
Content to breathe his native air,
    In his own ground.

Whose herds with milk, whose fields with bread,
  Whose flocks supply him with attire,
Whose trees in summer yield him shade,
    In winter fire.

Blest, who can unconcernedly find
  Hours, days, and years slide soft away,
In health of body, peace of mind,
    Quiet by day,

Sound sleep by night; study and ease,
  Together mixed; sweet recreation;
And innocence, which most does please
    With meditation.

Till the conversion of the Jews.
My vegetable love should grow
Vaster than empires, and more slow;
An hundred years should go to praise
Thine eyes and on thy forehead gaze;
Two hundred to adore each breast;
But thirty thousand to the rest;
An age at least to every part,
And the last age should show your heart;
For, Lady, you deserve this state,
Nor would I love at lower rate.
  But at my back I always hear
Time's winged chariot hurrying near;
And yonder all before us lie
Deserts of vast eternity.
Thy beauty shall no more be found,
Nor, in thy marble vault, shall sound
My echoing song: then worms shall try
That long preserved virginity,
And your quaint honour turn to dust,
And into ashes all my lust:
The grave's a fine and private place,
But none, I think, do there embrace.
  Now therefore, while the youthful hue
Sits on thy skin like morning dew,
And while thy willing soul transpires
At every pore with instant fires,
Now let us sport us while we may,
And now, like amorous birds of prey,
Rather at once our time devour
Than languish in his slow-chapt[1] power.
Let us roll all our strength and all
Our sweetness up into one ball,
And tear our pleasures with rough strife
Through the iron gates of life:
Thus, though we cannot make our sun
Stand still, yet we will make him run.

---

[1] *slow-chapt*] slowly devouring.

JOHN DRYDEN (1631–1700)

Poet and dramatist John Dryden was the leading literary figure of the late seventeenth century. He was appointed poet laureate in 1668, and two years later historiographer royal. The following is one of Dryden's most popular poems.

A Song for St. Cecilia's Day

1

From harmony, from heavenly harmony
  This universal frame began:
  When Nature underneath a heap
    Of jarring atoms lay,
  And could not heave her head,
The tuneful voice was heard from high:
  "Arise, ye more than dead."

Then cold, and hot, and moist, and dry,
In order to their stations leap,
  And Music's power obey.
From harmony, from heavenly harmony
  This universal frame began:
  From harmony to harmony
Through all the compass of the notes it ran,
The diapason closing full in man.

2

What passion cannot Music raise and quell!
  When Jubal struck the corded shell,
  His listening brethren stood around,
  And, wondering, on their faces fell
  To worship that celestial sound.
Less than a god they thought there could not dwell
  Within the hollow of that shell
  That spoke so sweetly and so well.
What passion cannot Music raise and quell!

3

The trumpet's loud clangor
  Excites us to arms,
With shrill notes of anger,
  And mortal alarms.
The double double double beat
  Of the thundering drum
Cries: "Hark! the foes come;
Charge, charge, 'tis too late to retreat."

4

The soft complaining flute
In dying notes discovers
The woes of hopeless lovers,
Whose dirge is whispered by the warbling lute.

5

Sharp violins proclaim
Their jealous pangs, and desperation,
Fury, frantic indignation,
Depth of pains, and height of passion,
  For the fair, disdainful dame.

6

But O! what art can teach,
  What human voice can reach,
The sacred organ's praise?
  Notes inspiring holy love,
Notes that wing their heavenly ways
  To mend the choirs above.

7

Orpheus could lead the savage race;
And trees unrooted left their place,
  Sequacious of the lyre;

Thus let me live, unseen, unknown;
Thus unlamented let me die;
Steal from the world, and not a stone
Tell where I lie.

WILLIAM BLAKE (1757–1827)

An important visionary artist who published vividly illustrated editions of his writings, and one of the most original of English poets, Blake was dismissed as a madman in his day. In addition to short poems of unmatched inspiration, he wrote lengthy and difficult verse prophecies.

The Tyger

Tyger! Tyger! burning bright
In the forests of the night,
What immortal hand or eye
Could frame thy fearful symmetry?

In what distant deeps or skies
Burnt the fire of thine eyes?
On what wings dare he aspire?
What the hand dare seize the fire?

And what shoulder, & what art,
Could twist the sinews of thy heart?
And when thy heart began to beat,
What dread hand? & what dread feet?

What the hammer? what the chain?
In what furnace was thy brain?
What the anvil? what dread grasp
Dare its deadly terrors clasp?

When the stars threw down their spears,
And water'd heaven with their tears,
Did he smile his work to see?
Did he who made the Lamb make thee?

Tyger! Tyger! burning bright
In the forests of the night,
What immortal hand or eye
Dare frame thy fearful symmetry?

London

I wander thro' each charter'd street, A
Near where the charter'd Thames does flow, B
And mark in every face I meet A
Marks of weakness, marks of woe. B

Imagery In every cry of every Man, A
In every Infant's cry of fear, B
In every voice, in every ban, A
The mind-forg'd manacles I hear. B

Dark, ominous, scary
How the Chimney-sweeper's cry A
Every black'ning Church appalls; B
And the hapless Soldier's sigh A
Runs in blood down Palace walls. B

But most thro' midnight streets I hear A
How the youthful Harlot's curse B
Blasts the new born Infant's tear, A
And blights with plagues the Marriage hearse. B

ROBERT BURNS (1759–1796)

The national poet of Scotland, Burns is best known for colorful, often humorous songs and poems written in the dialect of his homeland. Though largely self-educated, Burns was a meticulous craftsman who was a master of complex literary forms.

A Red, Red Rose

O, my luve is like *simile* a red, red rose, A
That's newly sprung in June. B
O, my luve is like the melodie, C
That's sweetly played in tune. B

archaic spelling As fair art thou, my bonnie lass, A
So deep in luve am I, B
And I will luve thee still, my dear, C
Till a' the seas gang dry. B

Imagery Till a' the seas gang dry, my dear, A
And the rocks melt wi' the sun! B
And I will luve thee still, my dear, C
While the sands o' life shall run. B

And fare thee weel, my only luve, *A*
And fare thee weel awhile! *B A*
And I will come again, my luve, *A*
Tho' it were ten thousand mile! *B*

My Heart's in the Highlands

Farewell to the Highlands, farewell to the North, *A*
The birth-place of valor, the country of worth! *A*
Wherever I wander, wherever I rove, *B*
The hills of the Highlands for ever I love. *B*

11 syllables

My heart's in the Highlands, my heart is not here, *A*
Repetition My heart's in the Highlands a-chasing the deer, *A*
A-chasing the wild deer and following the roe— *B*
My heart's in the Highlands, wherever I go. *B*

Farewell to the mountains high-covered with snow, *A*
Farewell to the straths and green valleys below, *A*
Farewell to the forests and wild-hanging woods, *B*
Farewell to the torrents and loud-pouring floods! *B*

My heart's in the Highlands, my heart is not here, *A*
My heart's in the Highlands a-chasing the deer, *A*
A-chasing the wild deer and following the roe— *B*
My heart's in the Highlands, wherever I go! *B*

WILLIAM WORDSWORTH (1770–1850)

Wordsworth was a pioneering figure of the Romantic movement and is one of English literature's major poets. Although he was viewed in his later life as a symbol of complacency by younger writers, his greatest works are masterpieces of eloquent passion.

Upon Westminster Bridge

Earth has not anything to show more fair: *A*
Dull would he be of soul who could pass by *B*
A sight so touching in its majesty: *B*
This City now doth, like a garment, wear *A*
The beauty of the morning: silent, bare, *A*
Ships, towers, domes, theatres, and temples lie *B*
Open unto the fields and to the sky; *B*
All bright and glittering in the smokeless air. *A*
Never did sun more beautifully steep *C*

In his first splendour, valley, rock, or hill; D
Ne'er saw I, never felt, a calm so deep! C
The river glideth at his own sweet will: D
Dear God! the very houses seem asleep; C
And all that mighty heart is lying still! D

Strange Fits of Passion Have I Known

Positive

Strange fits of passion have I known: A
And I will dare to tell, B
But in the Lover's ear alone, A
What once to me befel. B

Simile

When she I loved looked every day A   8 syll.
Fresh as a rose in June, B   6 syll.
I to her cottage bent my way, A
Beneath an evening moon. B

Upon the moon I fixed my eye, A
All over the wide lea; B

With quickening pace my horse drew nigh A
Those paths so dear to me. B

And now we reached the orchard-plot; A
And, as we climbed the hill, B
The sinking moon to Lucy's cot A
Came near, and nearer still. B

In one of those sweet dreams I slept, A
Kind Nature's gentlest boon! B
And all the while my eyes I kept A
On the descending moon. B

My horse moved on; hoof after hoof A
He raised, and never stopped: B
When down behind the cottage roof, A
At once, the bright moon dropped. B

Negative

What fond and wayward thoughts will slide A
Into a Lover's head! B
"O mercy!" to myself I cried, A
"If Lucy should be dead!" B

Daffodils

I wandered lonely as a cloud A
Natural That floats on high o'er vales and hills, B
imagery When all at once I saw a crowd, A
A host, of golden daffodils; B
Beside the lake, beneath the trees, A
Fluttering and dancing in the breeze. C

Continuous as the stars that shine A
And twinkle on the milky way, B
They stretched in never-ending line A
Along the margin of a bay: B
Ten thousand saw I at a glance, C
Tossing their heads in sprightly dance. C

Emphasis The waves beside them danced; but they A
Out-did the sparkling waves in glee: B
A poet could not but be gay, A
In such a jocund company: B
I gazed—and gazed—but little thought C
What wealth the show to me had brought: C

For oft, when on my couch I lie A
In vacant or in pensive mood, B
They flash upon that inward eye A
Which is the bliss of solitude; B
structure And then my heart with pleasure fills, C
And dances with the daffodils. C

My Heart Leaps Up

My heart leaps up when I behold A
A rainbow in the sky: B
Always So was it when my life began; A
positive So is it now I am a man; A
So be it when I shall grow old, A
Or let me die! B
The Child is father of the Man; A
And I could wish my days to be B
Bound each to each by natural piety. B

The World Is Too Much with Us

Direct
approach

The world is too much with us; late and soon, A
Getting and spending, we lay waste our powers: B
Little we see in Nature that is ours; B
We have given our hearts away, a sordid boon! A
The Sea that bares her bosom to the moon; A
The winds that will be howling at all hours, B
And are up-gathered now like sleeping flowers; B
For this, for everything, we are out of tune; A
Allusion   It moves us not.—Great God! I'd rather be C
A Pagan suckled in a creed outworn; D
So might I, standing on this pleasant lea, C
Have glimpses that would make me less forlorn; D
Greek   Have sight of Proteus rising from the sea; C
Allusion   Or hear old Triton blow his wreathèd horn. D

SAMUEL TAYLOR COLERIDGE (1772–1834)

A close associate of Wordsworth, Coleridge was similarly one of the leading Romantic poets, as well as an important critic and essayist. His longtime narcotics addiction gave many of his works a fantastical quality: "Kubla Khan" was admittedly inspired by an opium dream.

Kubla Khan

In Xanadu did Kubla Khan A
A stately pleasure-dome decree: B
Where Alph, the sacred river, ran A
Through caverns measureless to man A
    Down to a sunless sea. B
So twice five miles of fertile ground A
With walls and towers were girdled round: A
And there were gardens bright with sinuous rills, B
Where blossomed many an incense-bearing tree; C
Imagery   And here were forests ancient as the hills, B
Enfolding sunny spots of greenery. C

But oh! that deep romantic chasm which slanted A
Down the green hill athwart a cedarn cover! B
Biblical   A savage place! as holy and enchanted A
As e'er beneath a waning moon was haunted C

By woman wailing for her demon-lover! *B* [Devil = allusion]

And from this chasm, with ceaseless turmoil seething, *A*

As if this earth in fast thick pants were breathing, *A*

A mighty fountain momently was forced: *B*

Amid whose swift half-intermitted burst *C*

Huge fragments vaulted like rebounding hail, *D*

Or chaffy grain beneath the thresher's flail: *D*

And 'mid these dancing rocks at once and ever *e*

It flung up momently the sacred river. *e*

Five miles meandering with a mazy motion

Through wood and dale the sacred river ran, ⌐ River Styx?

Then reached the caverns measureless to man,

And sank in tumult to a lifeless ocean:

And 'mid this tumult Kubla heard from far ⌐

Ancestral voices prophesying war!   ⌐ crusades?

   The shadow of the dome of pleasure

   Floated midway on the waves;

   Where was heard the mingled measure

   From the fountain and the caves.

It was a miracle of rare device,

A sunny pleasure-dome with caves of ice!

   A damsel with a dulcimer

   In a vision once I saw:

   It was an Abyssinian maid,

   And on her dulcimer she played,

   Singing of Mount Abora.

   Could I revive within me

   Her symphony and song,

   To such a deep delight 'twould win me,

That with music loud and long,

I would build that dome in air,

That sunny dome! those caves of ice!

And all who heard should see them there,

And all should cry, Beware! Beware!

His flashing eyes, his floating hair!

Weave a circle round him thrice,

And close your eyes with holy dread,

For he on honey-dew hath fed,

And drunk the milk of Paradise.

LEIGH HUNT (1784–1859)

Better remembered today as an associate of Byron, Shelley, and Keats than as a literary original, Hunt was a crusading London journalist notably active in labor reform circles.

Abou Ben Adhem

Abou Ben Adhem (may his tribe increase!)
Awoke one night from a deep dream of peace,
And saw, within the moonlight in his room,
Making it rich, and like a lily in bloom,
An angel writing in a book of gold:—
Exceeding peace had made Ben Adhem bold,
And to the presence in the room he said,
    "What writest thou?"—The vision rais'd its head,
And with a look made of all sweet accord,
Answer'd, "The names of those who love the Lord."
    "And is mine one?" asked Abou. "Nay, not so,"
Replied the angel. Abou spoke more low,
But cheerly still; and said, "I pray thee, then,
Write me as one that loves his fellow men."
    The angel wrote, and vanish'd. The next night
It came again with a great wakening light,
And show'd the names whom love of God had blest,
And lo! Ben Adhem's name led all the rest.

GEORGE GORDON, LORD BYRON (1788–1824)

The prototypical Romantic figure, as well known to contemporaries for his heroic and scandalous personal life as for his writings, Byron continues to represent tempestuous and contradictory qualities of genius, melancholy, courage, despair, and passion.

She Walks in Beauty

She walks in beauty, like the night
    Of cloudless climes and starry skies;
And all that's best of dark and bright
    Meet in her aspect and her eyes:
Thus mellow'd to that tender light
    Which heaven to gaudy day denies.

One shade the more, one ray the less, A
    Had half impair'd the nameless grace B
Which waves in every raven tress, A
    Or softly lightens o'er her face; B
Where thoughts serenely sweet express A
    How pure, how dear their dwelling-place. B

And on that cheek, and o'er that brow, A
    So soft, so calm, yet eloquent, B
The smiles that win, the tints that glow, A
    But tell of days in goodness spent, B
A mind at peace with all below, A
    A heart whose love is innocent! B   *Beauty / Innocence*

When We Two Parted

When we two parted A
    In silence and tears, B
Half broken-hearted A   *Brokenness*
    To sever for years, B
Pale grew thy cheek and cold, C
    Colder thy kiss; D
Truly that hour foretold C
    Sorrow to this. D

The dew of the morning A
    Sunk chill on my brow— B
It felt like the warning A
    Of what I feel now. B
Thy vows are all broken, C
    And light is thy fame; D
I hear thy name spoken, C
    And share in its shame. D

They name thee before me, A
    A knell to mine ear; B
A shudder comes o'er me— A
    Why wert thou so dear? B
They know not I knew thee, C
    Who knew thee too well— D
Long, long shall I rue thee, C
    Too deeply to tell. D

In secret we met—
   In silence I grieve,
That thy heart could forget,
   Thy spirit deceive.
If I should meet thee
   After long years,
How should I greet thee?—
   With silence and tears.

The Destruction of Sennacherib

The Assyrian came down like the wolf on the fold,   *Simile*   A
And his cohorts were gleaming in purple and gold;   A
And the sheen of their spears was like stars on the sea,   *Simile*   B
When the blue wave rolls nightly on deep Galilee.   B

Imagery

Like the leaves of the forest when Summer is green,   A
That host with their banners at sunset were seen: A
Like the leaves of the forest when Autumn hath blown,   B
That host on the morrow lay wither'd and strown.   B

For the Angel of Death spread his wings on the blast,   A
And breathed in the face of the foe as he pass'd;   A
And the eyes of the sleepers wax'd deadly and chill,   B
And their hearts but once heaved, and for ever grew still!   B

And there lay the steed with his nostril all wide,   A
But through it there roll'd not the breath of his pride: A
And the foam of his gasping lay white on the turf,   B
And cold as the spray of the rock-beating surf.   B

And there lay the rider distorted and pale,   A
With the dew on his brow and the rust on his mail;   A
And the tents were all silent, the banners alone,   B
The lances unlifted, the trumpet unblown.   B

And the widows of Ashur are loud in their wail,   A
And the idols are broke in the temple of Baal;   A
And the might of the Gentile, unsmote by the sword,   B
Hath melted like snow in the glance of the Lord!
                            B

So We'll Go No More a Roving

So we'll go no more a roving A
   So late into the night, B
Though the heart be still as loving, A
   And the moon be still as bright. B

For the sword outwears its sheath, A
   And the soul wears out the breast, B
And the heart must pause to breathe, A
   And Love itself have rest. B

Though the night was made for loving, A
   And the day returns too soon, B
Yet we'll go no more a roving A
   By the light of the moon. B

light connect w/ heart

PERCY BYSSHE SHELLEY (1792–1822)

Shelley was, like his friend Byron, a somewhat larger-than-life Romantic who embodied—as well as helped determine—the rebellious spirit of his era. By the time of his death by drowning at age twenty-nine, he had composed a body of work of unequaled range.

Ozymandias

I met a traveller from an antique land A
Who said: Two vast and trunkless legs of stone B
Stand in the desert . . . Near them, on the sand, A
Half sunk, a shattered visage lies, whose frown, C
And wrinkled lip, and sneer of cold command,
Tell that its sculptor well those passions read
Which yet survive, stamped on these lifeless things,
The hand that mocked them, and the heart that fed:
And on the pedestal these words appear:
"My name is Ozymandias, king of kings: *fear him*
Look on my works, ye Mighty, and despair!"
Nothing beside remains. Round the decay
Of that colossal wreck, boundless and bare
The lone and level sands stretch far away.

Ode to the West Wind

O wild West Wind, thou breath of Autumn's being,
Thou, from whose unseen presence the leaves dead
Are driven, like ghosts from an enchanter fleeing,

Yellow, and black, and pale, and hectic red,
Pestilence-stricken multitudes: O thou,
Who chariotest to their dark wintry bed

The wingèd seeds, where they lie cold and low,
Each like a corpse within its grave, until
Thine azure sister of the Spring shall blow

Her clarion o'er the dreaming earth, and fill
(Driving sweet buds like flocks to feed in air)
With living hues and odours plain and hill:

Wild Spirit, which art moving everywhere;
Destroyer and preserver; hear, oh, hear!

Thou on whose stream, mid the steep sky's commotion,
Loose clouds like earth's decaying leaves are shed,
Shook from the tangled boughs of Heaven and Ocean,

Angels of rain and lightning: there are spread
On the blue surface of thine aëry surge,
Like the bright hair uplifted from the head

Of some fierce Maenad, even from the dim verge
Of the horizon to the zenith's height,
The locks of the approaching storm. Thou dirge

Of the dying year, to which this closing night
Will be the dome of a vast sepulchre,
Vaulted with all thy congregated might

Of vapours, from whose solid atmosphere
Black rain, and fire, and hail will burst: oh, hear!

Thou who didst waken from his summer dreams
The blue Mediterranean, where he lay,
Lulled by the coil of his crystalline streams,

Beside a pumice isle in Baiae's bay,
And saw in sleep old palaces and towers
Quivering within the wave's intenser day,

All overgrown with azure moss and flowers
So sweet, the sense faints picturing them! Thou
For whose path the Atlantic's level powers

Cleave themselves into chasms, while far below
The sea-blooms and the oozy woods which wear
The sapless foliage of the ocean, know

Thy voice, and suddenly grow gray with fear,
And tremble and despoil themselves: oh, hear!

If I were a dead leaf thou mightest bear;
If I were a swift cloud to fly with thee;
A wave to pant beneath thy power, and share

The impulse of thy strength, only less free
Than thou, O uncontrollable! If even
I were as in my boyhood, and could be

The comrade of thy wanderings over Heaven,
As then, when to outstrip thy skiey speed
Scarce seemed a vision; I would ne'er have striven

As thus with thee in prayer in my sore need.
Oh, lift me as a wave, a leaf, a cloud!
I fall upon the thorns of life! I bleed!

A heavy weight of hours has chained and bowed
One too like thee: tameless, and swift, and proud.

Make me thy lyre, even as the forest is:
What if my leaves are falling like its own!
The tumult of thy mighty harmonies

Will take from both a deep, autumnal tone,
Sweet though in sadness. Be thou, Spirit fierce,
My spirit! Be thou me, impetuous one!

Drive my dead thoughts over the universe
Like withered leaves to quicken a new birth!
And, by the incantation of this verse,

Scatter, as from an unextinguished hearth
Ashes and sparks, my words among mankind!
Be through my lips to unawakened earth

The trumpet of a prophecy! O, Wind,
If Winter comes, can Spring be far behind?

rhetorical

When the Lamp Is Shatter'd

When the lamp is shatter'd
The light in the dust lies dead—
When the cloud is scatter'd,
The rainbow's glory is shed.
When the lute is broken,
Sweet tones are remember'd not;
When the lips have spoken,
Loved accents are soon forgot.

As music and splendour
Survive not the lamp and the lute,
The heart's echoes render
No song when the spirit is mute,
No song but sad dirges,
Like the wind through a ruin'd cell,
Or the mournful surges
That ring the dead seaman's knell.

When hearts have once mingled,
Love first leaves the well-built nest;
The weak one is singled
To endure what it once possess'd.
O Love! who bewailest
The frailty of all things here,
Why choose you the frailest
For your cradle, your home, and your bier?

Its passions will rock thee
As the storms rock the ravens on high;
Bright reason will mock thee
Like the sun from a wintry sky.
From thy nest every rafter
Will rot, and thine eagle home
Leave thee naked to laughter,
When leaves fall and cold winds come.

Music, When Soft Voices Die

Music, when soft voices die,
Vibrates in the memory—
Odours, when sweet violets sicken,
Live within the sense they quicken.

Rose leaves, when the rose is dead,
Are heap'd for the beloved's bed;
And so thy thoughts, when thou art gone,
Love itself shall slumber on.

JOHN KEATS (1795–1821)

In his short life Keats developed a distinctive poetic style of precocious maturity. His poetry and letters contain profound insights into the nature of beauty, art, suffering, mortality, and other perennial issues.

On First Looking into Chapman's Homer

Much have I travell'd in the realms of gold,
    And many goodly states and kingdoms seen;
    Round many western islands have I been
Which bards in fealty to Apollo hold.
Oft of one wide expanse had I been told
    That deep-brow'd Homer ruled as his demesne;
    Yet did I never breathe its pure serene
Till I heard Chapman[1] speak out loud and bold:
Then felt I like some watcher of the skies
    When a new planet swims into his ken;
Or like stout Cortez when with eagle eyes
    He star'd at the Pacific—and all his men
Look'd at each other with a wild surmise—
    Silent, upon a peak in Darien.

When I Have Fears That I May Cease To Be

When I have fears that I may cease to be
    Before my pen has glean'd my teeming brain,
Before high-piled books, in charactery,
    Hold like rich garners the full ripen'd grain;
When I behold, upon the night's starr'd face,
    Huge cloudy symbols of a high romance,
And think that I may never live to trace
    Their shadows, with the magic hand of chance;

---

[1] *Chapman*] George Chapman (c. 1559–1634), Elizabethan poet famed for his translations of the epic poems of Homer.

And when I feel, fair creature of an hour,
    That I shall never look upon thee more,
Never have relish in the faery power
    Of unreflecting love;—then on the shore
Of the wide world I stand alone, and think
Till love and fame to nothingness do sink.

Bright Star, Would I Were Steadfast as Thou Art

Bright Star, would I were steadfast as thou art—
Not in lone splendour hung aloft the night,
And watching, with eternal lids apart,
Like Nature's patient sleepless Eremite,
The moving waters at their priest-like task
Of pure ablution round earth's human shores,
Or gazing on the new soft-fallen mask
Of snow upon the mountains and the moors—
No—yet still steadfast, still unchangeable,
Pillow'd upon my fair love's ripening breast,
To feel for ever its soft fall and swell,
Awake for ever in a sweet unrest,
    Still, still to hear her tender-taken breath,
    And so live ever—or else swoon to death.

Ode on a Grecian Urn

Thou still unravish'd bride of quietness,
    Thou foster-child of silence and slow time,
Sylvan historian, who canst thus express
    A flowery tale more sweetly than our rhyme:
What leaf-fring'd legend haunts about thy shape
    Of deities or mortals, or of both,
        In Tempe or the dales of Arcady?
    What men or gods are these? What maidens loth?
What mad pursuit? What struggle to escape?
        What pipes and timbrels? What wild ecstasy?

Heard melodies are sweet, but those unheard
    Are sweeter; therefore, ye soft pipes, play on;
Not to the sensual ear, but, more endear'd,

Pipe to the spirit ditties of no tone:
Fair youth, beneath the trees, thou canst not leave
   Thy song, nor ever can those trees be bare;
     Bold Lover, never, never canst thou kiss,
Though winning near the goal—yet, do not grieve;
   She cannot fade, though thou hast not thy bliss,
     For ever wilt thou love, and she be fair!

Ah, happy, happy boughs! that cannot shed
   Your leaves, nor ever bid the Spring adieu;
And, happy melodist, unwearied,
   For ever piping songs for ever new;
More happy love! more happy, happy love!
   For ever warm and still to be enjoy'd,
     For ever panting, and for ever young;
All breathing human passion far above,
   That leaves a heart high-sorrowful and cloy'd,
     A burning forehead, and a parching tongue.

Who are these coming to the sacrifice?
   To what green altar, O mysterious priest,
Lead'st thou that heifer lowing at the skies,
   And all her silken flanks with garlands drest?
What little town by river or sea shore,
   Or mountain-built with peaceful citadel,
     Is emptied of this folk, this pious morn?
And, little town, thy streets for evermore
   Will silent be; and not a soul to tell
     Why thou art desolate, can e'er return.

O Attic shape! Fair attitude! with brede
   Of marble men and maidens overwrought,
With forest branches and the trodden weed;
   Thou, silent form, dost tease us out of thought
As doth eternity: Cold Pastoral!
   When old age shall this generation waste,
     Thou shalt remain, in midst of other woe
Than ours, a friend to man, to whom thou say'st,
   "Beauty is truth, truth beauty,"—that is all
     Ye know on earth, and all ye need to know.

ELIZABETH BARRETT BROWNING (1806–1861)

The most famous female English poet of her day, Browning was married to poet Robert Browning, for whom she wrote the famous sonnet sequence *Sonnets from the Portuguese,* the romantic themes of which are embodied in the following selections.

Sonnet 6

Go from me. Yet I feel that I shall stand
Henceforward in thy shadow. Nevermore
Alone upon the threshold of my door
Of individual life I shall command
The uses of my soul, nor lift my hand
Serenely in the sunshine as before,
Without the sense of that which I forbore—
Thy touch upon the palm. The widest land
Doom takes to part us, leaves thy heart in mine
With pulses that beat double. What I do
And what I dream include thee, as the wine
Must taste of its own grapes. And when I sue
God for myself, He hears that name of thine,
And sees within my eyes the tears of two.

Sonnet 43

How do I love thee? Let me count the ways.
I love thee to the depth and breadth and height
My soul can reach, when feeling out of sight
For the ends of Being and ideal Grace.
I love thee to the level of everyday's
Most quiet need, by sun and candle-light.
I love thee freely, as men strive for Right;
I love thee purely, as they turn from Praise.
I love thee with the passion put to use
In my old griefs, and with my childhood's faith.
I love thee with a love I seemed to lose
With my lost saints,—I love thee with the breath,
Smiles, tears, of all my life!—and, if God choose,
I shall but love thee better after death.

ALFRED, LORD TENNYSON (1809–1892)

Tennyson was the most famous and respected English poet of the Victorian era. Poet laureate from 1850 until his death, he served as the literary voice of an empire. "The Charge of the Light Brigade" was inspired by a tragic battle during the Crimean War.

The Charge of the Light Brigade

Half a league, half a league,
Half a league onward,
All in the valley of Death
   Rode the six hundred.
"Forward the Light Brigade!
Charge for the guns!" he said.
Into the valley of Death
   Rode the six hundred.

"Forward, the Light Brigade!"
Was there a man dismay'd?
Not tho' the soldier knew
   Some one had blunder'd.
Theirs not to make reply,
Theirs not to reason why,
Theirs but to do and die.
Into the valley of Death
   Rode the six hundred.

Cannon to right of them,
Cannon to left of them,
Cannon in front of them
   Volley'd and thunder'd;
Storm'd at with shot and shell,
Boldly they rode and well,
Into the jaws of Death,
Into the mouth of hell
   Rode the six hundred.

Flash'd all their sabres bare,
Flash'd as they turn'd in air
Sabring the gunners there,

Charging an army, while
   All the world wonder'd.
Plunged in the battery-smoke
Right thro' the line they broke;
Cossack and Russian
Reel'd from the sabre-stroke
   Shatter'd and sunder'd.
Then they rode back, but not,
   Not the six hundred.

Cannon to right of them,
Cannon to left of them,
Cannon behind them
   Volley'd and thunder'd;
Storm'd at with shot and shell,
While horse and hero fell,
They that had fought so well
Came thro' the jaws of Death,
Back from the mouth of hell,
All that was left of them,
   Left of six hundred.

When can their glory fade?
O the wild charge they made!
   All the world wonder'd.
Honour the charge they made!
Honour the Light Brigade,
   Noble six hundred!

Crossing the Bar

Sunset and evening star,
   And one clear call for me!
And may there be no moaning of the bar,
   When I put out to sea,

But such a tide as moving seems asleep,
   Too full for sound and foam,
When that which drew from out the boundless deep
   Turns again home.

Twilight and evening bell,
   And after that the dark!
And may there be no sadness of farewell,
   When I embark;

For tho' from out our bourne of Time and Place
   The flood may bear me far,
I hope to see my Pilot face to face
   When I have crost the bar.

Ulysses

It little profits that an idle king,
By this still hearth, among these barren crags,
Matched with an aged wife, I mete and dole
Unequal laws unto a savage race,
That hoard, and sleep, and feed, and know not me.
I cannot rest from travel; I will drink
Life to the lees. All times I have enjoyed
Greatly, have suffered greatly, both with those
That loved me, and alone; on shore, and when
Through scudding drifts the rainy Hyades
Vexed the dim sea. I am become a name;
For always roaming with a hungry heart
Much have I seen and known—cities of men
And manners, climates, councils, governments,
Myself not least, but honoured of them all—
And drunk delight of battle with my peers,
Far on the ringing plains of windy Troy.
I am a part of all that I have met;
Yet all experience is an arch wherethrough
Gleams that untraveled world whose margin fades
Forever and forever when I move.
How dull it is to pause, to make an end,
To rust unburnished, not to shine in use!
As though to breathe were life! Life piled on life
Were all too little, and of one to me
Little remains; but every hour is saved
From that eternal silence, something more,

A bringer of new things; and vile it were
For some three suns to store and hoard myself,
And this grey spirit yearning in desire
To follow knowledge like a sinking star,
Beyond the utmost bound of human thought.

   This is my son, mine own Telemachus,
To whom I leave the scepter and the isle—
Well-loved of me, discerning to fulfill
This labour, by slow prudence to make mild
A rugged people, and through soft degrees
Subdue them to the useful and the good.
Most blameless is he, centered in the sphere
Of common duties, decent not to fail
In offices of tenderness, and pay
Meet adoration to my household gods,
When I am gone. He works his work, I mine.

   There lies the port; the vessel puffs her sail;
There gloom the dark, broad seas. My mariners,
Souls that have toiled, and wrought, and thought with me—
That ever with a frolic welcome took
The thunder and the sunshine, and opposed
Free hearts, free foreheads—you and I are old;
Old age hath yet his honour and his toil.
Death closes all; but something ere the end,
Some work of noble note, may yet be done,
Not unbecoming men that strove with gods.
The lights begin to twinkle from the rocks;
The long day wanes; the slow moon climbs; the deep
Moans round with many voices. Come, my friends,
'Tis not too late to seek a newer world.
Push off, and sitting well in order smite
The sounding furrows; for my purpose holds
To sail beyond the sunset, and the baths
Of all the western stars, until I die.
It may be that the gulfs will wash us down;
It may be we shall touch the Happy Isles,
And see the great Achilles, whom we knew.
Though much is taken, much abides; and though

We are not now that strength which in old days
Moved earth and heaven, that which we are, we are—
One equal temper of heroic hearts,
Made weak by time and fate, but strong in will
To strive, to seek, to find, and not to yield.

Break, Break, Break

Break, break, break,
  On thy cold gray stones, O Sea!
And I would that my tongue could utter
  The thoughts that arise in me.

O, well for the fisherman's boy,
  That he shouts with his sister at play!
O, well for the sailor lad,
  That he sings in his boat on the bay!

And the stately ships go on
  To their haven under the hill;
But O for the touch of a vanished hand,
  And the sound of a voice that is still!

Break, break, break,
  At the foot of thy crags, O Sea!
But the tender grace of a day that is dead
  Will never come back to me.

Tears, Idle Tears

Tears, idle tears, I know not what they mean,
Tears from the depth of some divine despair
Rise in the heart, and gather to the eyes,
In looking on the happy autumn-fields,
And thinking of the days that are no more.

Fresh as the first beam glittering on a sail,
That brings our friends up from the underworld,
Sad as the last which reddens over one
That sinks with all we love below the verge;
So sad, so fresh, the days that are no more.

Ah, sad and strange as in dark summer dawns
The earliest pipe of half-awakened birds
To dying ears, when unto dying eyes
The casement slowly grows a glimmering square;
So sad, so strange, the days that are no more.

Dear as remembered kisses after death,
And sweet as those by hopeless fancy feigned
On lips that are for others; deep as love,
Deep as first love, and wild with all regret;
O Death in Life, the days that are no more!

O, Yet We Trust that Somehow Good

O, yet we trust that somehow good
    Will be the final goal of ill,
    To pangs of nature, sins of will,
Defects of doubt, and taints of blood;

That nothing walks with aimless feet;
    That not one life shall be destroyed,
    Or cast as rubbish to the void,
When God hath made the pile complete;

That not a worm is cloven in vain;
    That not a moth with vain desire
    Is shriveled in a fruitless fire,
Or but subserves another's gain.

Behold, we know not anything;
    I can but trust that good shall fall
    At last—far off—at last, to all,
And every winter change to spring.

So runs my dream; but what am I?
    An infant crying in the night;
    An infant crying for the light,
And with no language but a cry.

Flower in the Crannied Wall

Flower in the crannied wall,
I pluck you out of the crannies,
I hold you here, root and all, in my hand,

Optimism in spite of loss

Little flower—but *if* I could understand
What you are, root and all, and all in all,
I should know what God and man is.

ROBERT BROWNING (1812–1889)

Although he stands with Tennyson as one of the seminal Victorian poets, Browning enjoyed little of his counterpart's public success until late in his life. He is today best remembered for perfectly wrought dramatic monologues such as "My Last Duchess."

My Last Duchess

FERRARA

That's my last Duchess painted on the wall,
Looking as if she were alive. I call
That piece a wonder, now: Frà Pandolf's hands
Worked busily a day, and there she stands.
Will 't please you sit and look at her? I said
"Frà Pandolf" by design: for never read
Strangers like you that pictured countenance,
The depth and passion of its earnest glance,
But to myself they turned (since none puts by
The curtain I have drawn for you, but I)
And seemed as they would ask me, if they durst,
How such a glance came there; so, not the first
Are you to turn and ask thus. Sir, 't was not
Her husband's presence only, called that spot
Of joy into the Duchess' cheek: perhaps
Frà Pandolf chanced to say "Her mantle laps
Over my lady's wrist too much," or "Paint
Must never hope to reproduce the faint
Half-flush that dies along her throat": such stuff
Was courtesy, she thought, and cause enough
For calling up that spot of joy. She had
A heart—how shall I say?—too soon made glad,
Too easily impressed; she liked whate'er
She looked on, and her looks went everywhere.
Sir, 't was all one! My favour at her breast,
The dropping of the daylight in the West,

The bough of cherries some officious fool
Broke in the orchard for her, the white mule
She rode with round the terrace—all and each
Would draw from her alike the approving speech,
Or blush, at least. She thanked men,—good! but thanked
Somehow—I know not how—as if she ranked
My gift of a nine-hundred-years-old name
With anybody's gift. Who'd stoop to blame
This sort of trifling? Even had you skill
In speech—(which I have not)—to make your will
Quite clear to such an one, and say, "Just this
Or that in you disgusts me; here you miss,
Or there exceed the mark"—and if she let
Herself be lessoned so, nor plainly set
Her wits to yours, forsooth, and made excuse,
—E'en then would be some stooping; and I choose
Never to stoop. Oh sir, she smiled, no doubt,
Whene'er I passed her; but who passed without
Much the same smile? This grew; I gave commands;
Then all smiles stopped together. There she stands
As if alive. Will 't please you rise? We'll meet
The company below, then. I repeat,
The Count your master's known munificence
Is ample warrant that no just pretence
Of mine for dowry will be disallowed;
Though his fair daughter's self, as I avowed
At starting, is my object. Nay, we'll go
Together down, sir. Notice Neptune, though,
Taming a sea-horse, thought a rarity,
Which Claus of Innsbruck cast in bronze for me!

Home-Thoughts, from Abroad

Oh, to be in England
Now that April's there,
And whoever wakes in England
Sees, some morning, unaware,
That the lowest boughs and the brushwood sheaf
Round the elm-tree bole are in tiny leaf,
While the chaffinch sings on the orchard bough
In England—now!

And after April, when May follows,
And the whitethroat builds, and all the swallows!
Hark, where my blossomed peartree in the hedge
Leans to the field and scatters on the clover
Blossoms and dewdrops—at the bent spray's edge—
That's the wise thrush; he sings each song twice over,
Lest you should think he never could recapture
The first fine careless rapture!
And though the fields look rough with hoary dew,
All will be gay when noontide wakes anew
The buttercups, the little children's dower
—Far brighter than this gaudy melon-flower!

MATTHEW ARNOLD (1822–1888)

One of the most influential critics of the mid-Victorian Age, Arnold also created important poetic works. The most famous of these, "Dover Beach," has come to be seen as one of the seminal expressions of the spirit of Arnold's time.

Dover Beach

The sea is calm to-night, *—Nostalgic tone*
The tide is full, the moon lies fair
Upon the Straits;—on the French coast, the light
Gleams, and is gone; the cliffs of England stand,
Glimmering and vast, out in the tranquil bay.
Come to the window, sweet is the night air!
Only, from the long line of spray
Where the ebb meets the moon-blanch'd sand,
Listen! you hear the grating roar
Of pebbles which the waves suck back, and fling,
At their return, up the high strand,
Begin, and cease, and then again begin,
With tremulous cadence slow, and bring
The eternal note of sadness in.

Sophocles long ago
Heard it on the Aegaean, and it brought
Into his mind the turbid ebb and flow
Of human misery; we   *Struggle between*
Find also in the sound a thought, *spiritual and secular*
Hearing it by this distant northern sea.

The sea of faith
Was once, too, at the full, and round earth's shore
Lay like the folds of a bright girdle furl'd;
But now I only hear
Its melancholy, long, withdrawing roar,
Retreating to the breath
Of the night-wind down the vast edges drear
And naked shingles of the world.

Ah, love, let us be true
To one another! for the world, which seems
To lie before us like a land of dreams,
So various, so beautiful, so new,
Hath really neither joy, nor love, nor light,
Nor certitude, nor peace, nor help for pain;
And we are here as on a darkling plain
Swept with confused alarms of struggle and flight,
Where ignorant armies clash by night.

DANTE GABRIEL ROSSETTI (1828–1882)

This poet and painter was one of the founders of the Pre-Raphaelite Brother-
hood, a group of young artists, writers, and critics striving to bring back truth to
nature. Rossetti's poetry was said to be full of lewd sensuality and came under
some harsh criticism causing him to eventually have a mental breakdown. The
following is a popular monorhythmic stanza.

The Woodspurge

The wind flapped loose, the wind was still,
Shaken out dead from tree and hill:
I had walked on at the wind's will,—
I sat now, for the wind was still.

Between my knees my forehead was,—
My lips, drawn in, said not Alas!
My hair was over in the grass,
My naked ears heard the day pass.

My eyes, wide open, had the run
Of some ten weeds to fix upon;
Among those few, out of the sun,
The woodspurge flowered, three cups in one.

From perfect grief there need not be
Wisdom or even memory:
One thing then learnt remains to me,—
The woodspurge has a cup of three.

GEORGE MEREDITH (1828–1909)

As the author of *The Ordeal of Richard Feverel* and *The Egoist*, Meredith is gener-
ally considered more important as a novelist than as a poet. He did, however,
produce a large quantity of excellent verse, held in high regard by critics and
scholars. This sonnet is among the most anthologized poems.

Lucifer in Starlight

On a starred night Prince Lucifer uprose.
Tired of his dark dominion swung the fiend
Above the rolling ball in cloud part screened,
Where sinners hugged their spectre of repose.
Poor prey to his hot fit of pride were those.
And now upon his western wing he leaned,
Now his huge bulk o'er Afric's sands careened,
Now the black planet shadowed Arctic snows.
Soaring through wider zones that pricked his scars
With memory of the old revolt from Awe,
He reached a middle height, and at the stars,
Which are the brain of heaven, he looked, and sank.
Around the ancient track marched, rank on rank,
The army of unalterable law.

CHRISTINA ROSSETTI (1830–1894)

Sister of Pre-Raphaelite painter and poet Dante Gabriel Rossetti, Christina
Rossetti wrote verses that combined the sensuality of her aesthetic heritage with
a fervent commitment to the Anglican faith. "Remember" is from her haunting
fairytale in verse, *Goblin Market*.

A Birthday

My heart is like a singing bird
    Whose nest is in a water'd shoot;
My heart is like an apple-tree
    Whose boughs are bent with thick-set fruit;

My heart is like a rainbow shell
   That paddles in a halcyon sea;
My heart is gladder than all these,
   Because my love is come to me.

Raise me a daïs of silk and down;
   Hang it with vair and purple dyes;
Carve it in doves and pomegranates,
   And peacocks with a hundred eyes;
Work it in gold and silver grapes,
   In leaves and silver fleurs-de-lys;
Because the birthday of my life
   Is come, my love is come to me.

Remember

Remember me when I am gone away,
   Gone far away into the silent land;
   When you can no more hold me by the hand,
Nor I half turn to go yet turning stay.
Remember me when no more day by day
   You tell me of our future that you planned:
   Only remember me; you understand
It will be late to counsel then or pray.
Yet if you should forget me for a while
   And afterwards remember, do not grieve:
   For if the darkness and corruption leave
   A vestige of the thoughts that once I had,
Better by far you should forget and smile
   Than that you should remember and be sad.

LEWIS CARROLL (1832–1898)

Immortalized as the author of *Alice's Adventures in Wonderland,* "Lewis Carroll" was the pseudonym of Oxford mathematician Charles Lutwidge Dodgson. "Jabberwocky," probably the most celebrated nonsense poem in English, first appeared in *Alice's* sequel, *Through the Looking-Glass and What Alice Found There* (1871).

Jabberwocky

'Twas brillig, and the slithy toves
   Did gyre and gimble in the wabe:
All mimsy were the borogoves,
   And the mome raths outgrabe.

"Beware the Jabberwock, my son!
    The jaws that bite, the claws that catch!
Beware the Jubjub bird, and shun
    The frumious Bandersnatch!"

He took his vorpal sword in hand:
    Long time the manxome foe he sought—
So rested he by the Tumtum tree,
    And stood awhile in thought.

And, as in uffish thought he stood,
    The Jabberwock, with eyes of flame,
Came whiffling through the tulgey wood,
    And burbled as it came!

One, two! One, two! And through and through
    The vorpal blade went snicker-snack!
He left it dead, and with its head
    He went galumphing back.

"And hast thou slain the Jabberwock?
    Come to my arms, my beamish boy!
O frabjous day! Callooh! Callay!"
    He chortled in his joy.

'Twas brillig, and the slithy toves
    Did gyre and gimble in the wabe:
All mimsy were the borogoves,
    And the mome raths outgrabe.

WILLIAM MORRIS (1834–1896)

This businessman, poet, artist, weaver, and furniture designer was one of the busiest men of the Victorian era. In fact, many of his poems were written while he was weaving. This verse is from *The Earthly Paradise* (1868), a collection of classical myths and legends.

An Apology

    Of Heaven or Hell I have no power to sing,
I cannot ease the burden of your fears,
Or make quick-coming death a little thing,
Or bring again the pleasure of past years,
Nor for my words shall ye forget your tears,
Or hope again for aught that I can say,
The idle singer of an empty day.

But rather, when, aweary of your mirth,
From full hearts still unsatisfied ye sigh,
And, feeling kindly unto all the earth,
Grudge every minute as it passes by,
Made the more mindful that the sweet days die—
Remember me a little then, I pray,
The idle singer of an empty day.

The heavy trouble, the bewildering care
That weighs us down who live and earn our bread,
These idle verses have no power to bear;
So let me sing of names rememberèd,
Because they, living not, can ne'er be dead,
Or long time take their memory quite away
From us poor singers of an empty day.

Dreamer of dreams, born out of my due time,
Why should I strive to set the crooked straight?
Let it suffice me that my murmuring rhyme
Beats with light wing against the ivory gate,
Telling a tale not too importunate
To those who in the sleepy region stay,
Lulled by the singer of an empty day.

Folk say a wizard to a northern king
At Christmastide such wondrous things did show,
That through one window men beheld the spring,
And through another saw the summer glow,
And through a third the fruited vines a-row,
While still, unheard, but in its wonted way,
Piped the drear wind of that December day.

So with this Earthly Paradise it is,
If ye will read aright, and pardon me,
Who strive to build a shadowy isle of bliss
Midmost the beating of the steely sea,
Where tossed about all hearts of men must be;
Whose ravening monsters mighty men shall slay,
Not the poor singer of an empty day.

ALGERNON CHARLES SWINBURNE (1837–1909)

Swinburne was a master of poetic meter whose passionate verse was denounced by the Victorian public, leaving quite an impact on English lyric poetry. This passage was selected from *Poems and Ballads* (1866), which contained many of these controversial pieces.

Love and Sleep

Lying asleep between the strokes of night
  I saw my love lean over my sad bed,
  Pale as the duskiest lily's leaf or head,
Smooth-skinned and dark, with bare throat made to bite,
Too wan for blushing and too warm for white,
  But perfect-coloured without white or red.
  And her lips opened amorously, and said—
I wist not what, saving one word—Delight.
And all her face was honey to my mouth,
  And all her body pasture to mine eyes;
    The long lithe arms and hotter hands than fire,
The quivering flanks, hair smelling of the south,
  The bright light feet, the splendid supple thighs
    And glittering eyelids of my soul's desire.

THOMAS HARDY (1840–1928)

Having established a place for himself among the greatest English novelists, Hardy turned to poetry late in his career; nonetheless, his verses achieved a rare distinction and have exerted a wide influence.

Hap

If but some vengeful god would call to me
From up the sky, and laugh: "Thou suffering thing,
Know that thy sorrow is my ecstasy,
That thy love's loss is my hate's profiting!"
Then would I bear it, clench myself, and die,
Steeled by the sense of ire unmerited;
Half-eased in that a Powerfuller than I
Had willed and meted me the tears I shed.

But not so. How arrives it joy lies slain,
And why unblooms the best hope ever sown?
—Crass Casualty obstructs the sun and rain,
And dicing Time for gladness casts a moan. . . .
These purblind Doomsters had as readily strown
Blisses about my pilgrimage as pain.

GERARD MANLEY HOPKINS (1844–1889)

A Jesuit priest, Hopkins never published during his lifetime. His idiosyncratic poems exhibit technical and linguistic innovations that still seem daring, and reflect their author's passionate spiritual life.

God's Grandeur

The world is charged with the grandeur of God.
  It will flame out, like shining from shook foil;
  It gathers to a greatness, like the ooze of oil
Crushed. Why do men then now not reck his rod?
Generations have trod, have trod, have trod;
  And all is seared with trade; bleared, smeared with toil;
  And wears man's smudge and shares man's smell: the soil
Is bare now, nor can foot feel, being shod.

And for all this, nature is never spent;
  There lives the dearest freshness deep down things;
And though the last lights off the black West went
  Oh, morning, at the brown brink eastward, springs—
Because the Holy Ghost over the bent
  World broods with warm breast and with ah! bright wings.

Hurrahing in Harvest

Summer ends now; now, barbarous in beauty, the stooks[1] rise
Around; up above, what wind-walks! what lovely behavior
Of silk-sack clouds! has wilder, wilful-wavier
Meal-drift moulded ever and melted across skies?

---

[1] *stooks*] sheaves of grain.

I walk, I lift up, I lift up heart, eyes,
Down all that glory in the heavens to glean our Saviour;
And, éyes, héart, what looks, what lips yet gave you a
Rapturous love's greeting of realer, of rounder replies?

And the azurous hung hills are his world-wielding shoulder
Majestic—as a stallion stalwart, very-violet-sweet!—
These things, these things were here and but the beholder
Wanting; which two when they once meet,
The heart rears wings bold and bolder
And hurls for him, O half hurls earth for him off under his feet.

ROBERT BRIDGES (1844–1930)

This former physician and poet laureate was an advocate of spelling reform and
cofounded the Society for Pure English. He was a master at prosody and in his
collection *New Verse* (1925) he experimented with meter based on syllables
instead of accents. English composers set many of his poems to music.

Nightingales

Beautiful must be the mountains whence ye come,
And bright in the fruitful valleys the streams, wherefrom
        Ye learn your song:
Where are those starry woods? O might I wander there,
    Among the flowers, which in that heavenly air
        Bloom the year long!

Nay, barren are those mountains and spent the streams:
Our song is the voice of desire, that haunts our dreams,
        A throe of the heart,
Whose pining visions dim, forbidden hopes profound,
    No dying cadence nor long sigh can sound,
        For all our art.

Alone, aloud in the raptured ear of men
    We pour our dark nocturnal secret; and then,
        As night is withdrawn
From these sweet-springing meads and bursting boughs of May,
    Dream, while the innumerable choir of day
        Welcome the dawn.

WILLIAM ERNEST HENLEY (1849–1903)

Henley was an editor of a number of periodicals in London that introduced the public to young writers like Kipling, Wells, and Yeats. He spent many years in crippling pain, due to tuberculosis of the bone. Many of his poems reflect on some of his hospital experiences. This is one of Henley's most famous poems.

Invictus

[handwritten: Optimism in spite of loss]

Out of the night that covers me,
　　Black as the Pit from pole to pole,
I thank whatever gods may be
　　For my unconquerable soul.

In the fell clutch of circumstance
　　I have not winced nor cried aloud.
Under the bludgeonings of chance
　　My head is bloody, but unbowed.

Beyond this place of wrath and tears
　　Looms but the Horror of the shade,
And yet the menace of the years
　　Finds, and shall find, me unafraid.

It matters not how strait the gate,
　　How charged with punishments the scroll,
I am the master of my fate;
　　I am the captain of my soul.

ROBERT LOUIS STEVENSON (1850–1894)

The author of *Treasure Island* and other widely read works, Stevenson spent most of his life traveling the world in an effort to overcome his chronic tuberculosis. "Requiem" is carved onto the poet's gravestone in Samoa.

Requiem

Under the wide and starry sky
Dig the grave and let me lie;
Glad did I live and gladly die,
And I laid me down with a will.

> This be the verse you grave for me:
> *Here he lies where he longed to be;*
> *Home is the sailor, home from the sea,*
> *And the hunter home from the hill.*

A. E. HOUSMAN (1859–1936)

Housman was a noted British Latin scholar whose poems combined simplicity and craft in a manner that found favor with both critics and the reading public.

To an Athlete Dying Young

Nostalgic

The time you won your town the race
We chaired you through the market-place;
Man and boy stood cheering by,
And home we brought you shoulder-high.

Optimistic

To-day, the road all runners come,
Shoulder-high we bring you home,
And set you at your threshold down,
Townsman of a stiller town.

Smart lad, to slip betimes away
From fields where glory does not stay
And early though the laurel grows
It withers quicker than the rose.

Eyes the shady night has shut
Cannot see the record cut,
And silence sounds no worse than cheers
After earth has stopped the ears: *secular vs. spiritual*

Now you will not swell the rout
Of lads that wore their honours out,
Runners whom renown outran
And the name died before the man.

So set, before its echoes fade,
The fleet foot on the sill of shade,
And hold to the low lintel up
The still-defended challenge-cup.

And round that early-laurelled head
Will flock to gaze the strengthless dead,
And find unwithered on its curls
The garland briefer than a girl's.

Loveliest of Trees

Loveliest of trees, the cherry now
Is hung with bloom along the bough,
And stands about the woodland ride
Wearing white for Eastertide.

Now, of my threescore years and ten,
Twenty will not come again,
And take from seventy springs a score,
It only leaves me fifty more.

And since to look at things in bloom
Fifty springs are little room,
About the woodlands I will go
To see the cherry hung with snow.

When I Was One-and-Twenty

When I was one-and-twenty
    I heard a wise man say,
"Give crowns and pounds and guineas
    But not your heart away;
Give pearls away and rubies
    But keep your fancy free."
But I was one-and-twenty,
    No use to talk to me.

When I was one-and-twenty
    I heard him say again,
"The heart out of the bosom
    Was never given in vain;
'Tis paid with sighs a plenty
    And sold for endless rue."
And I am two-and-twenty,
    And oh, 'tis true, 'tis true.

RUDYARD KIPLING (1865–1936)

An author who achieved distinction and enormous popularity with his fiction and verses, Kipling remains the essential voice of late-Victorian colonialism. Despite radical shifts in public taste since that era, his writings continue to attract readers by their sheer excellence.

Gunga Din

You make talk o' gin and beer
When you're quartered safe out 'ere,
An' you're sent to penny-fights an' Aldershot[1] it;
But when it comes to slaughter
You will do your work on water,
An' you'll lick the bloomin' boots of 'im that's got it.
Now in Injia's sunny clime,
Where I used to spend my time
A-servin' of 'Er Majesty the Queen,
Of all them blackfaced crew
The finest man I knew
Was our regimental bhisti,[2] Gunga Din.
      He was "Din! Din! Din!
You limping lump o' brick-dust, Gunga Din!
      Hi! slippery hitherao!
      Water, get it! Panee lao![3]
You squidgy-nosed old idol, Gunga Din."

The uniform 'e wore
Was nothin' much before,
An' rather less than 'arf o' that be'ind,
For a piece o' twisty rag
An' a goatskin water-bag
Was all the field-equipment 'e could find.
When the sweatin' troop-train lay
In a sidin' through the day,
Where the 'eat would make your bloomin' eyebrows crawl,
We shouted "Harry By!"[4]

---

[1] *Aldershot*] military camp near London.
[2] *bhisti*] water carrier.
[3] *Panee lao*] Bring water swiftly.
[4] *Harry By*] enlisted man's equivalent for "O brother."

Till our throats were bricky-dry,
Then we wopped 'im 'cause 'e couldn't serve us all.
      It was "Din! Din! Din!
You 'eathen, where the mischief 'ave you been?
      You put some juldee[5] in it
      Or I'll marrow[6] you this minute
If you don't fill up my helmet, Gunga Din!"

'E would dot an' carry one
Till the longest day was done;
An' 'e didn't seem to know the use o' fear.
If we charged or broke or cut,
You could bet your bloomin' nut,
'E'd be waitin' fifty paces right flank rear.
With 'is mussick[7] on 'is back,
'E would skip with our attack,
An' watch us till the bugles made "Retire,"
An' for all 'is dirty 'ide
'E was white, clear white, inside
When 'e went to tend the wounded under fire!
      It was "Din! Din! Din!"
With the bullets kickin' dust-spots on the green.
      When the cartridges ran out,
      You could hear the front-files shout,
"Hi! ammunition-mules an' Gunga Din!"

I sha'n't forgit the night
When I dropped be'ind the fight
With a bullet where my belt-plate should 'a' been.
I was chokin' mad with thirst,
An' the man that spied me first
Was our good old grinnin', gruntin' Gunga Din.
'E lifted up my 'ead,
An' he plugged me where I bled,
An' 'e guv me 'arf-a-pint o' water-green:
It was crawlin' and it stunk,
But of all the drinks I've drunk,
I'm gratefullest to one from Gunga Din.
      It was "Din! Din! Din!"

---

[5] *juldee*] be quick.
[6] *marrow*] hit.
[7] *mussick*] water skin.

'Ere's a beggar with a bullet through 'is spleen;
     'E's chawin' up the ground,
      An' 'e's kickin' all around:
For Gawd's sake git the water, Gunga Din!

'E carried me away
To where a dooli[8] lay,
An' a bullet come an' drilled the beggar clean.
'E put me safe inside,
An' just before 'e died:
"I 'ope you liked your drink," sez Gunga Din.
So I'll meet 'im later on
At the place where 'e is gone—
Where it's always double drill and no canteen;
'E'll be squattin' on the coals,
Givin' drink to poor damned souls,
An' I'll get a swig in hell from Gunga Din!
       Yes, Din! Din! Din!
You Lazarushian-leather[9] Gunga Din!
      Though I've belted you and flayed you,
      By the living Gawd that made you,
You're a better man than I am, Gunga Din!

Recessional

(A Victorian Ode)

God of our fathers, known of old—
    Lord of our far-flung battle line—
Beneath whose awful hand we hold
    Dominion over palm and pine—
Lord God of Hosts, be with us yet,
Lest we forget—lest we forget!

The tumult and the shouting dies—
    The Captains and the Kings depart—
Still stands Thine ancient sacrifice,
    An humble and a contrite heart.
Lord God of Hosts, be with us yet,
Lest we forget—lest we forget!

---

[8] *dooli*] stretcher.
[9] *Lazarushian-leather*] humourous combination of "Lazarus" and "Russian leather."

Far-called our navies melt away—
   On dune and headland sinks the fire—
Lo, all our pomp of yesterday
   Is one with Nineveh and Tyre!
Judge of the Nations, spare us yet,
Lest we forget—lest we forget!

If, drunk with sight of power, we loose
   Wild tongues that have not Thee in awe—
Such boastings as the Gentiles use,
   Or lesser breeds without the Law—
Lord God of Hosts, be with us yet,
Lest we forget—lest we forget!

For heathen heart that puts her trust
   In reeking tube and iron shard—
All valiant dust that builds on dust,
                And guarding calls not Thee to guard.
              For frantic boast and foolish word,
              Thy Mercy on Thy People, Lord!
                       Amen.

If

If you can keep your head when all about you
   Are losing theirs and blaming it on you,
If you can trust yourself when all men doubt you,
   but make allowance for their doubting too;
If you can wait and not be tired by waiting,
   Or being lied about, don't deal in lies,
Or being hated don't give way to hating,
   And yet don't look too good, nor talk too wise:

If you can dream—and not make dreams your master;
   If you can think—and not make thoughts your aim,
If you can meet with Triumph and Disaster
   And treat those two impostors just the same;
If you can bear to hear the truth you've spoken
   Twisted by knaves to make a trap for fools,
Or watch the things you gave your life to, broken,
   And stoop and build 'em up with worn-out tools:

If you can make one heap of all your winnings
   And risk it on one turn of pitch-and-toss,
And lose, and start again at your beginnings

And never breathe a word about your loss;
If you can force your heart and nerve and sinew
    To serve your turn long after they are gone,
And so hold on when there is nothing in you
    Except the Will which says to them: "Hold on!"

If you can talk with crowds and keep your virtue,
    Or walk with Kings—nor lose the common touch,
If neither foes nor loving friends can hurt you,
    If all men count with you, but none too much;
If you can fill the unforgiving minute
    With sixty seconds' worth of distance run,
Yours is the Earth and everything that's in it,
    And—which is more—you'll be a Man, my son!

WILLIAM BUTLER YEATS (1865–1939)

Perhaps the most distinguished poet of the early twentieth century, Yeats fused elements of his Irish heritage with a modern temperament to create a matchless body of moving, well-wrought verse.

The Wild Swans at Coole

The trees are in their autumn beauty,
The woodland paths are dry,
Under the October twilight the water
Mirrors a still sky;
Upon the brimming water among the stones
Are nine-and-fifty swans.

The nineteenth autumn has come upon me
Since I first made my count;
I saw, before I had well finished,
All suddenly mount
And scatter wheeling in great broken rings
Upon their clamorous wings.

I have looked upon those brilliant creatures,
And now my heart is sore.
All's changed since I, hearing at twilight,
The first time on this shore,
The bell-beat of their wings above my head,
Trod with a lighter tread.

Unwearied still, lover by lover,
They paddle in the cold
Companionable streams or climb the air;
Their hearts have not grown old;
Passion or conquest, wander where they will,
Attend upon them still.

But now they drift on the still water,
Mysterious, beautiful;
Among what rushes will they build,
By what lake's edge or pool
Delight men's eyes when I awake some day
To find they have flown away?

Easter 1916

I have met them at close of day
Coming with vivid faces
From counter or desk among grey
Eighteenth-century houses.
I have passed with a nod of the head
Or polite meaningless words,
Or have lingered awhile and said
Polite meaningless words,
And thought before I had done
Of a mocking tale or a gibe
To please a companion
Around the fire at the club,
Being certain that they and I
But lived where motley is worn:
All changed, changed utterly:
A terrible beauty is born.

That woman's days were spent
In ignorant good-will,
Her nights in argument
Until her voice grew shrill.
What voice more sweet than hers
When, young and beautiful,
She rode to harriers?
This man had kept a school
And rode our wingèd horse;
This other his helper and friend
Was coming into his force;

He might have won fame in the end,
So sensitive his nature seemed,
So daring and sweet his thought.
This other man I had dreamed
A drunken, vainglorious lout.
He had done most bitter wrong
To some who are near my heart,
Yet I number him in the song;
He, too, has resigned his part
In the casual comedy;
He, too, has been changed in his turn,
Transformed utterly:
A terrible beauty is born.

Hearts with one purpose alone
Through summer and winter seem
Enchanted to a stone
To trouble the living stream.
The horse that comes from the road,
The rider, the birds that range
From cloud to tumbling cloud,
Minute by minute they change;
A shadow of cloud on the stream
Changes minute by minute;
A horse-hoof slides on the brim,
And a horse plashes within it;
The long-legged moor-hens dive,
And hens to moor-cocks call;
Minute by minute they live:
The stone's in the midst of all.

Too long a sacrifice
Can make a stone of the heart.
O when may it suffice?
That is Heaven's part, our part
To murmur name upon name,
As a mother names her child
When sleep at last has come
On limbs that had run wild.
What is it but nightfall?
No, no, not night but death;
Was it needless death after all?
For England may keep faith
For all that is done and said.

We know their dream; enough
   To know they dreamed and are dead;
And what if excess of love
   Bewildered them till they died?
I write it out in a verse—
   MacDonagh and MacBride
And Connolly and Pearse
Now and in time to be,
   Wherever green is worn,
Are changed, changed utterly:
   A terrible beauty is born.

WALTER DE LA MARE (1873–1956)

De la Mare began his career as a writer while being employed as an accountant for an oil company. His works included prose fiction and nonfiction stories—many of them for children—but he is best known for his poetry. His success came after publishing his collection of poems, *The Listeners* (1912).

The Listeners

"Is there anybody there?" said the Traveller,
   Knocking on the moonlit door;
And his horse in the silence champ'd the grasses
   Of the forest's ferny floor:
And a bird flew up out of the turret,
   Above the Traveller's head:
And he smote upon the door again a second time;
   "Is there anybody there?" he said.
But no one descended to the Traveller;
   No head from the leaf-fringed sill
Lean'd over and look'd into his grey eyes,
   Where he stood perplex'd and still.
But only a host of phantom listeners
   That dwelt in the lone house then
Stood listening in the quiet of the moonlight
   To that voice from the world of men:
Stood thronging the faint moonbeams on the dark stair,
   That goes down to the empty hall,
Hearkening in an air stirr'd and shaken
   By the lonely Traveller's call.
And he felt in his heart their strangeness,
   Their stillness answering his cry,

While his horse moved, cropping the dark turf,
   'Neath the starr'd and leafy sky;
For he suddenly smote on the door, even
   Louder, and lifted his head:—
"Tell them I came, and no one answer'd,
   That I kept my word," he said.
Never the least stir made the listeners,
   Though every word he spake
Fell echoing through the shadowiness of the still house
   From the one man left awake:
Ay, they heard his foot upon the stirrup,
   And the sound of iron on stone,
And how the silence surged softly backward,
   When the plunging hoofs were gone.

EDWARD THOMAS (1878–1917)

Thomas was a successful reviewer and critic, but it wasn't until he received some encouragement from Robert Frost that he began to write poetry. In his work he reflected on the beauty of nature and the English countryside. He composed war poems while serving in World War I, and eventually lost his life at the Battle of Arras.

The Owl

Downhill I came, hungry, and yet not starved;
Cold, yet had heat within me that was proof
Against the North wind; tired, yet so that rest
Had seemed the sweetest thing under a roof.

Then at the inn I had food, fire, and rest,
Knowing how hungry, cold, and tired was I.
All of the night was quite barred out except
An owl's cry, a most melancholy cry

Shaken out long and clear upon the hill,
No merry note, nor cause of merriment,
But one telling me plain what I escaped
And others could not, that night, as in I went.

And salted was my food, and my repose,
Salted and sobered, too, by the bird's voice
Speaking for all who lay under the stars,
Soldiers and poor, unable to rejoice.

JOHN MASEFIELD (1878–1967)

This "Poet of the Sea" spent many years on the water in hopes of becoming a merchant marine officer, but due to an illness had to return to the mainland. He was a playwright, novelist, and poet whose many works tell of his days at sea.

Cargoes

Quinquireme of Nineveh from distant Ophir
Rowing home to haven in sunny Palestine,
With a cargo of ivory,
And apes and peacocks,
Sandalwood, cedarwood, and sweet white wine.

Stately Spanish galleon coming from the Isthmus,
Dipping through the Tropics by the palm-green shores,
With a cargo of diamonds,
Emeralds, amethysts,
Topazes, and cinnamon, and gold moidores.

Dirty British coaster with a salt-caked smoke-stack,
Butting through the Channel in the mad March days,
With a cargo of Tyne coal,
Road-rails, pig-lead,
Firewood, iron-ware, and cheap tin trays.

Sea Fever

I must go down to the seas again, to the lonely sea and the sky,
And all I ask is a tall ship and a star to steer her by;
And the wheel's kick and the wind's song and the white sail's shaking,
And a grey mist on the sea's face, and a grey dawn breaking.

I must go down to the seas again, for the call of the running tide
Is a wild call and a clear call that may not be denied;
And all I ask is a windy day with the white clouds flying,
And the flung spray and the blown spume, and the sea-gulls crying.

I must go down to the seas again, to the vagrant gypsy life,
To the gull's way and the whale's way where the wind's like a whetted
    knife;
And all I ask is a merry yarn from a laughing fellow-rover,
And quiet sleep and a sweet dream when the long trick's over.

D. H. LAWRENCE (1885–1930)

This novelist, poet, and essayist was one of the greatest figures in twentieth century English literature. He came under controversy after publishing his fourth novel, *The Rainbow* (1915), and was prosecuted for obscenity. Many of his works are of views and experiences that reflect his own life as in "Snake," one of his most anthologized poems.

Snake

A snake came to my water trough
On a hot, hot day, and I in pajamas for the heat,
To drink there.

In the deep, strange-scented shade of the great dark carob tree
I came down the steps with my pitcher
And must wait, must stand and wait, for there he was at the trough
   before me.

He reached down from a fissure in the earth-wall in the gloom
And trailed his yellow-brown slackness soft-bellied down, over the edge
   of the stone trough
And rested his throat upon the stone bottom,
And where the water had dripped from the tap, in a small clearness,
He sipped with his straight mouth,
Softly drank through his straight gums, into his slack long body,
Silently.

Someone was before me at my water trough,
And I, like a second-comer, waiting.

He lifted his head from his drinking, as cattle do,
And looked at me vaguely, as drinking cattle do,
And flickered his two-forked tongue from his lips, and mused a
   moment,
And stooped and drank a little more,
Being earth-brown, earth-golden from the burning bowels of the
   earth
On the day of Sicilian July, with Etna smoking.

The voice of my education said to me
He must be killed,
For in Sicily the black, black snakes are innocent, the gold are
   venomous.
And voices in me said, If you were a man
You would take a stick and break him now, and finish him off.

But I must confess how I liked him,
How glad I was he had come like a guest in quiet, to drink at my
    water trough
And depart peaceful, pacified, and thankless
Into the burning bowels of this earth?

Was it cowardice, that I dared not kill him?
Was it perversity, that I longed to talk to him?
Was it humility, to feel so honored?
I felt so honored.

And yet those voices:
If you were not afraid, you would kill him!

And truly I was afraid, I was most afraid,
But even so, honored still more
That he should seek my hospitality
From out the dark door of the secret earth.

He drank enough
And lifted his head, dreamily, as one who has drunken,
And flickered his tongue like a forked night on the air, so black,
Seeming to lick his lips,
And looked around like a god, unseeing, into the air,
And slowly turned his head,
And slowly, very slowly, as if thrice adream
Proceeded to draw his slow length curving round
And climb the broken bank of my wall-face.

And as he put his head into that dreadful hole,
And as he slowly drew up, snake-easing his shoulders, and entered
    further,
A sort of horror, a sort of protest against his withdrawing into that
    horrid black hole,
Deliberately going into the blackness, and slowly drawing himself after,
Overcame me now his back was turned.

I looked round, I put down my pitcher,
I picked up a clumsy log
And threw it at the water trough with a clatter.

I think it did not hit him;
But suddenly that part of him that was left behind convulsed in
    undignified haste,

Writhed like lightning, and was gone
Into the black hole, the earth-lipped fissure in the wall-front
At which, in the intense still noon, I stared with fascination.

And immediately I regretted it.
I thought how paltry, how vulgar, what a mean act!
I despised myself and the voices of my accursed human education.

And I thought of the albatross,
And I wished he would come back, my snake.

For he seemed to me again like a king,
Like a king in exile, uncrowned in the underworld,
Now due to be crowned again.

And so, I missed my chance with one of the lords
Of life.
And I have something to expiate:
A pettiness.

RUPERT BROOKE (1887–1915)

This poet started off his literary career writing about the English countryside and way of life. In 1914, Brooke was commissioned into the Royal Navy and turned his focus to writing patriotic poems. His life was cut short one year later after getting blood poisoning. "The Soldier" is from the sonnet sequence *1914 and Other Poems* (1915), which was published posthumously.

The Soldier

If I should die, think only this of me:
   That there's some corner of a foreign field
That is for ever England. There shall be
   In that rich earth a richer dust concealed;
A dust whom England bore, shaped, made aware,
   Gave, once, her flowers to love, her ways to roam,
A body of England's, breathing English air,
   Washed by the rivers, blest by suns of home.

And think, this heart, all evil shed away,
   A pulse in the eternal mind, no less

Gives somewhere back the thoughts by England given;
Her sights and sounds; dreams happy as her day;
And laughter, learnt of friends; and gentleness,
In hearts at peace, under an English heaven.

T. S. ELIOT (1888–1965)

This poet, critic, and playwright was a great influence on twentieth century poetry and was awarded the Nobel Prize for Literature in 1948. He wrote approximately 600 articles and reviews during his lifetime and was the founder and editor of *The Criterion,* an influential quarterly review.

Sweeney Among the Nightingales

ὤμοι, πέπληγμαι καιρίαν πληγὴν ἔσω.

Apeneck Sweeney spreads his knees
Letting his arms hang down to laugh,
The zebra stripes along his jaw
Swelling to maculate giraffe.

The circles of the stormy moon
Slide westward toward the River Plate,
Death and the Raven drift above
And Sweeney guards the horned gate.

Gloomy Orion and the Dog
Are veiled; and hushed the shrunken seas;
The person in the Spanish cape
Tries to sit on Sweeney's knees

Slips and pulls the table cloth
Overturns a coffee-cup,
Reorganized upon the floor
She yawns and draws a stocking up;

The silent man in mocha brown
Sprawls at the window-sill and gapes;
The waiter brings in oranges
Bananas figs and hothouse grapes;

The silent vertebrate in brown
Contracts and concentrates, withdraws;
Rachel *née* Rabinovitch
Tears at the grapes with murderous paws;

She and the lady in the cape
Are suspect, thought to be in league;
Therefore the man with heavy eyes
Declines the gambit, shows fatigue,

Leaves the room and reappears
Outside the window, leaning in,
Branches of wistaria
Circumscribe a golden grin;

The host with someone indistinct
Converses at the door apart,
The nightingales are singing near
The Convent of the Sacred Heart,

And sang within the bloody wood
When Agamemnon cried aloud,
And let their liquid siftings fall
To stain the stiff dishonoured shroud.

ISAAC ROSENBERG (1890–1918)

Although he wrote about other subjects, Rosenberg was best known for his poetry that tells of his experiences as a private during World War I. He detested the war, and after serving almost four years died in action at the age of twenty-eight. This is considered one of his finest war poems.

Returning, We Hear the Larks

Sombre the night is.
And though we have our lives, we know
What sinister threat lurks there.

Dragging these anguished limbs, we only know
This poison-blasted track opens on our camp—
On a little safe sleep.

But hark! joy—joy—strange joy.
Lo! heights of night ringing with unseen larks.
Music showering on our upturned list'ning faces.

Death could drop from the dark
As easily as song—
But song only dropped,
Like a blind man's dreams on the sand
By dangerous tides,
Like a girl's dark hair for she dreams no ruin lies there,
Or her kisses where a serpent hides.

WILFRED OWEN (1893–1918)

Owen was one of the most technically innovative and influential of all the World
War I poets. His work expressed the horrors and cruelty of war, and many of his
poems have been set to music. He lost his life on the Western Front one week
before the armistice.

Anthem for Doomed Youth

What passing-bells for these who die as cattle?
    —Only the monstrous anger of the guns.
    Only the stuttering rifles' rapid rattle
Can patter out their hasty orisons.
No mockeries now for them; no prayers nor bells;
    Nor any voice of mourning save the choirs,—
The shrill, demented choirs of wailing shells;
And bugles calling for them from sad shires.

What candles may be held to speed them all?
    Not in the hands of boys but in their eyes
Shall shine the holy glimmers of goodbyes.
    The pallor of girls' brows shall be their pall;
Their flowers the tenderness of patient minds,
And each slow dusk a drawing-down of blinds.

Greater Love

Red lips are not so red
    As the stained stones kissed by the English dead.
Kindness of wooed and wooer

Seems shame to their love pure.
O Love, your eyes lose lure
    When I behold eyes blinded in my stead!

Your slender attitude
    Trembles not exquisite like limbs knife-skewed,
Rolling and rolling there
Where God seems not to care;
Till the fierce Love they bear
    Cramps them in death's extreme decrepitude.

Your voice sings not so soft,—
    Though even as wind murmuring through raftered loft,—
Your dear voice is not dear,
Gentle, and evening clear,
As theirs whom none now hear,
    Now earth has stopped their piteous mouths that coughed.

Heart, you were never hot,
    Nor large, nor full like hearts made great with shot;
And though your hand be pale,
Paler are all which trail
Your cross through flame and hail:
    Weep, you may weep, for you may touch them not.

ROBERT GRAVES (1895–1985)

Graves fought in some of the most brutal battles of World War I. His wartime
experiences have been compiled into two volumes of powerful poetry, *Over the
Brazier* (1916) and *Fairies and Fusiliers* (1917).

When I'm Killed

When I'm killed, don't think of me
Buried there in Cambrin Wood,
Nor as in Zion think of me
With the Intolerable Good.
And there's one thing that I know well,
I'm damned if I'll be damned to Hell!

So when I'm killed, don't wait for me,
Walking the dim corridor;
In Heaven or Hell, don't wait for me,

Or you must wait for evermore.
You'll find me buried, living-dead
In these verses that you've read.

So when I'm killed, don't mourn for me,
Shot, poor lad, so bold and young,
Killed and gone—don't mourn for me.
On your lips my life is hung:
O friends and lovers, you can save
Your playfellow from the grave.

W. H. AUDEN (1907–1973)

A Briton who emigrated to the United States on the eve of World War II, Auden
produced a large body of first-quality verse. "Musée des Beaux Arts" was inspired
by a painting by Pieter Brueghel the Elder in the Royal Museum of Fine Arts
in Brussels.

Musée des Beaux Arts

About suffering they were never wrong,
The Old Masters: how well they understood
Its human position; how it takes place
While someone else is eating or opening a window or just walking
    dully along;
How, when the aged are reverently, passionately waiting
For the miraculous birth, there always must be
Children who did not specially want it to happen, skating
On a pond at the edge of the wood:
They never forgot
That even the dreadful martyrdom must run its course
Anyhow in a corner, some untidy spot
Where the dogs go on with their doggy life and the torturer's horse
Scratches its innocent behind on a tree.

In Brueghel's *Icarus,* for instance: how everything turns away
Quite leisurely from the disaster; the plowman may
Have heard the splash, the forsaken cry,
But for him it was not an important failure; the sun shone
As it had to on the white legs disappearing into the green
Water; and the expensive delicate ship that must have seen
Something amazing, a boy falling out of the sky,
Had somewhere to get to and sailed calmly on.

STEPHEN SPENDER (1909–1995)

Spender responded to political and social injustice through his poetry. He also wrote short stories, a novel, translations, and sociological studies and was coeditor of two magazines. Spender was knighted in 1983. This is his most famous poem.

I Think Continually of Those Who Were Truly Great

I think continually of those who were truly great.
Who, from the womb, remembered the soul's history
Through corridors of light where the hours are suns,
Endless and singing. Whose lovely ambition
Was that their lips, still touched with fire,
Should tell of the spirit clothed from head to foot in song.
And who hoarded from the spring branches
The desires falling across their bodies like blossoms.

What is precious is never to forget
The delight of the blood drawn from ageless springs
Breaking through rocks in worlds before our earth;
Never to deny its pleasure in the simple morning light,
Nor its grave evening demand for love;
Never to allow gradually the traffic to smother
With noise and fog the flowering of the spirit.

Near the snow, near the sun, in the highest fields
See how those names are fêted by the waving grass,
And by the streamers of white cloud,
And whispers of wind in the listening sky;
The names of those who in their lives fought for life,
Who wore at their hearts the fire's centre.
Born of the sun they traveled a short while towards the sun,
And left the vivid air signed with their honour.

DYLAN THOMAS (1914–1953)

Welsh-born Thomas led a tempestuous life, dying from alcohol abuse before his fortieth birthday. His personal turmoil bore fruit, however, in a number of the undisputed masterworks of English-language poetry, including this unforgettable villanelle.

Do Not Go Gentle into That Good Night

Do not go gentle into that good night,
Old age should burn and rave at close of day;
Rage, rage against the dying of the light.

Though wise men at their end know dark is right,
Because their words had forked no lightning they
Do not go gentle into that good night.

Good men, the last wave by, crying how bright
Their frail deeds might have danced in a green bay,
Rage, rage against the dying of the light.

Wild men who caught and sang the sun in flight,
And learn, too late, they grieved it on its way,
Do not go gentle into that good night.

Grave men, near death, who see with blinding sight
Blind eyes could blaze like meteors and be gay,
Rage, rage against the dying of the light.

And you, my father, there on the sad height,
Curse, bless, me now with your fierce tears, I pray.
Do not go gentle into that good night.
Rage, rage against the dying of the light.

Alphabetical List of Titles

Alphabetical List of First Lines